Reducing Educational Disadvantage

Paul Widlake

Open University Press

Milton Keynes · Philadelphia

Open University Press
Open University Educational Enterprises Limited
12 Cofferidge Close
Stony Stratford
Milton Keynes MK11 1BY, England

and
242 Cherry Street
Philadelphia, PA 19106, USA

First published 1986

British Library Cataloguing in Publication Data

Widlake, Paul
  Reducing educational disadvantage.—
  (Innovations in education series)
  1. Community schools   2. School facilities
  —Extended use
  I. Title   II. Series
  370.19'4   LB2820

ISBN 0–335–15241–4
ISBN 0–335–15240–6 Pbk

370.32
W.ᴅ

Library of Congress Cataloging in Publication Data

Widlake, Paul.
  Reducing educational disadvantage.
  (Innovations in education)
  Includes index.
  1. Socially handicapped children—Education—Great
Britain.   2. Compensatory education—Great Britain.
3. Community and school—Great Britain.   4. Home and
school—Great Britain.   I. Title.   II. Series.
  LC4096.G7W48 1986   371.96'7'0941   86–8676

0027550

ISBN 0–335–15241–4
ISBN 0–335–15240–6 (pbk.)

132528

Typeset by S & S Press, Abingdon, Oxfordshire
Printed in Great Britain by J. W. Arrowsmith Ltd, Bristol.

Reducing Educational Disadvantage

Innovations in Education

Series Editor: Colin Fletcher (Lecturer in the School of Policy Studies, Cranfield Institute of Technology)

There have been periods of major innovation in public education. What do the achievements amount to and what are the prospects for progress now? There are issues in each slice of the education sector. How have the issues come about?

Each author analyses their own sphere, argues from experience and communicates clearly. Here are books that speak both with and for the teaching profession; books that can be shared with all those involved in the future of education.

Three quotations have helped to shape the series:

> The whole process – the false starts, frustrations, adaptions, the successive recasting of intentions, the detours and conflicts – needs to be comprehended. Only then can we understand what has been achieved and learn from experience.
>
> *Marris and Rein*

> In this time of considerable educational change and challenge the need for teachers to write has never been greater.
>
> *Hargreaves*

> A wise innovator should prepare packages of programmes and procedures which . . . could be put into effect quickly in periods of recovery and reorganisation following a disaster.
>
> *Hirsh*

CURRENT TITLES IN THE SERIES

Bernard Barker: *Rescuing the Comprehensive Experience*
Jan Stewart: *The Making of the Primary School*
Paul Widlake: *Reducing Educational Disadvantage*

Contents

Series editor's foreword   vii

Acknowledgements   viii

**Part one   From Compensatory Education to a
Communications Model**

  1 Personal perspective   1

  2 Historical perspective   9

  3 The communications model: an inner-city multicultural
    primary school   18

    Hamm Green School   18

    Turning the school round   20

    Factors in success   22

    A multicultural school?   24

  4 The communications model: group work in a day
    special school   26

    The Downton Park project   26

    Parental meetings   28

    Parental involvement in group work   31

  5 Joys and sorrows of home–school liaison work   33

    Muddle in the 1970s   33

    Confusion in the 1980s   36

    Conclusion   38

  6 Lessons to be learned from the communications model   40

    Complexity of the issues   41

    Is co-operation possible?   45

    Community education past and future   48

Part two Towards Participation

 7 Collaborative learning: a whole-system approach   55
   The Coventry Community Education Project (1969–85)   55
   Community schools and educational standards   59
 8 Parents, language and reading development   63
   How widespread is parent involvement?   64
   Goals and methods   65
   Problems and how they may be tackled   67
   So what's new?   68
 9 Through the suspicion barrier   77
   Ask the parents   77
   Example: Woden Primary   78
   Example: George Stephenson Primary   79
   Example: St Dominic's Infants School   80
   Example: Hazel Primary   82
   Reading project at Dean's Lane Infants   82
   Example: Sutton Centre   84
   Home–school liaison at Elm Hill Special School   86
   Home and school involvement in Salford and Leicester   91
10 Collaborative learning: small is beautiful?   103
   Neighbourhood Centre Project, North Humberside   103
   Pen Green Centre, Corby   109

Part three Ways Forward

11 What professionals might do about themselves   113
   Changes in attitude   116
   New approaches to learning and presentation   118
   Reconsidering 'parents'   119
   A new professionalism   120
12 What professionals might do with parents   124
   Continuity and partnership   125
   Women and children first?   127
   A school–family concordat   128
   Conclusion   130

Notes and references   132
Index   143

Series editor's foreword

The implied subtitle of this book is 'Educating with Parents'. Its aim is to show that the fourth 'R' is Relationships; the hard to teach are reached through the participation in learning of parents and community. This aim has been recognised for years, but Widlake is highly critical of how 'difficult children' and 'tough neighbourhoods' were first thought of as deficient and then, later, as diffident. He describes these approaches as the 'compensatory' and 'communications' models and vividly illustrates their insights and blind spots.

Widlake denies the educational validity of categories such as deprivation and IQ. His prime purpose is to depict and develop participation, and to this end he has been researching in dozens of schools, working alongside staff as they devise schemes. He accepts that some good practices may be adopted through a kind of spare-part surgery; but he urges the reader to appreciate the foundations of such schemes. From primary schools, secondary schools and a special school for maladjusted children come provisions and proofs – all of which show how innovations to reduce educational disadvantage in the 1980s are likely to gain in strength by 1990 and beyond. In conclusion he brings the pieces of innovation together in an account of community education.

Probably the most challenging chapters are those that ask. What should parents and professionals do next? Every concerned reader will value the clarity of Widlake's position just as much as his witnessing of so much good work. 'The lot of the innovator is likely to be a hard one,' he says. At the same time he shows how much has been achieved in community-based 'special-needs' and remedial education. This book is both a source of inspiration and a guide to methods of effective change.

Colin Fletcher

Acknowledgements

A book of this sort, drawing on projects pursued over a long period and in different educational establishments, accumulates many debts. I am grateful to colleagues in the teaching profession who have shared their experiences so readily. I hope what I have written conveys something of their own enthusiasm to others who have begun to feel jaded or doubtful of the value of their work.

Research assistants were appointed to most of the projects mentioned, and where publications have ensued I have acknowledged them in the appropriate places. The use of the material in this book is entirely my responsibility, as are the opinions, the good things and the not so good. All names of schools have been invented, except those that have published accounts of their work, and these I have quoted and referenced.

Colin Fletcher and the editorial staff at the Open University Press have been unfailingly helpful in the most practical and constructive manner. Such faults as remain in the book must be attributed to the author.

PART ONE

From Compensatory Education to a Communications Model

Sooner or later, false thinking brings wrong conduct.

Julian Huxley, *Essays of a Biologist*

CUSINS: Do you call poverty a crime?
UNDERSHAFT: The worst of crimes. All the other crimes are virtues beside it.

George Bernard Shaw, *Major Barbara*, Act iv

CHAPTER 1

Personal Perspective

The cause of popular education has been passionately argued in Britain since the end of the Second World War. My own career has, in a sense, followed the line of debate.

It began, by chance, in adult education, when I was in the Royal Air Force. I was given the task of running short courses, in a vast range of subjects, for such officers and other ranks as could persuade their commanding officers that they should be released from duty in order to broaden their minds. Whatever the effects on my students, there was no doubt that my mind broadened exponentially – but that would make another book. What most affected me as I tried to realise the awe-inspiring list of objectives for my one-month courses on history, English literature, 'civics' and philosophy was the vast range of attainment among men (and a few women) who were all roughly the same age. Some were functionally illiterate; here were men with all their senses intact, their wits fully about them, who had been to school for nine or ten years – just as I had – and yet could decipher only the simplest text in the crudest newspapers. In the 'school of life' they had picked up survival skills and advanced information and knowledge; but formal schooling had been to them, as to the young Laurie Lee, indistinguishable from a detention centre: 'a sour form of fiddling or prison labour, like picking oakum or sewing sacks'.[1]

This phenomenon set me pondering some of the questions that have engaged me throughout my educational career:

- What efforts have been made, and are being made, to improve the delivery of educational services to the mass of the population?
- Why do these efforts so conspicuously fail to enthuse so many pupils?

- Are there other programmes, comparatively untried, that provide models for further action?

I have recently written about older pupils;[2] in the present book, the emphasis is on younger children and parents. My justification for advancing views is that I am able to report excellent work from all over Britain that is producing positive results, including at last some hard data in support of the notion that 'the idea of the community school has powerful implications for community regeneration'[3].

This material has been accumulated from action–research projects that I have directed or participated in since joining A. H. Halsey's Educational Priority Areas (EPA) Project (1969–72). After that job, I worked on another for the Schools Council, looking at teaching materials for disadvantaged pupils; subsequently, from a post at Manchester Polytechnic, I continued the habit of action research as a means of providing a resource for my teacher training. During this period I undertook a longitudinal study of parental involvement in a day special school; fifteen teachers participated, writing accounts that served as one element in the requirements for a part-time honours B.Ed. Many threads were drawn together in this particular project. It meant visiting the homes of all pupils in this inner–city school for the educationally subnormal (to use the label then current); linking home and school through direct action on the part of teachers and other professionals; bringing parents into school (and the consequences of this course of action, many of them unanticipated); and inculcating the notion of school–based action research (involving both the local polytechnic and university) with a practical purpose and outcome.

Soon after, an opportunity was provided to evaluate another ambitious project located in a block of flats in a notorious area of Manchester. This was a determined effort by a dedicated team to improve relationships between parents and schools, under the most exacting conditions. There were many difficulties, but they were again not quite those that might have been anticipated. It proved feasible to involve parents. Towards the end of the project a group of women made strenuous and partly successful efforts to persuade the local authority to maintain it; and along the way they displayed a whole range of previously unused skills.

In the background, as it were, at Manchester Polytechnic we were running our regular and occasional courses. An authority then noted for its bold educational initiatives, Manchester decided to enlarge its team of home–school liaison teachers. We ran a course jointly with the authority, creating appropriate materials, placing the teachers in schools and using their experience to devise some of the course content; we discussed interpersonal relationships and tried to analyse situations where communication had broken down with staff or parents. Among the resources we could draw upon was another joint action–research project conducted by twelve teachers who examined aspects of work by an heroic home–school teacher in the Hulme area of the city. They wrote assignments, all of which were enthusiastic, about her work. There was thus a valuable build-up of shared experience.

During this period funds were provided for an ethnographic study of a primary school where the major population group was of Afro-Caribbean origin. We were able to identify effective and ineffective practice in home–school relations. We noted in particular the superficiality of some of the efforts to represent Caribbean culture and the lack of specific policies to help the children investigate their ethnicity; and we wondered whether the seeds of later disaffection were being sown. Our premonitions seemed to be well-founded, judging by the responses of some of the pupils when we followed their progress in secondary schools.

Since leaving Manchester Polytechnic I have been operating as an independent researcher and writer. I have continued to focus on the possibilities of improving pupils' performance in schools through the evolution of home–school relationships. A charitable trust commissioned a study of the role of a home–school liaison worker in a residential special school, where – despite my mental set against segregated education – it was possible to observe and record some first-class efforts to break down barriers and to bring parents into a close and productive relationship with the school; another study, replicating this one, was carried out for a neighbouring local authority (see Chapter 9).[4] To demonstrate my eagerness to be fair to the special schools, I have gathered data on four of them, and have observed one (Hamm Green) in some detail, over a period of nine years (see Chapter 3). I greatly admire the dedication and caring attitudes of the staffs; but I still believe that many of the problems that they strive, often successfully, to overcome, would not exist if their pupils were being helped within the mainstream school system.

Another and most enjoyable commission was an invitation to help the staff at the Sutton Centre in Nottinghamshire to evaluate their home-visiting programme, one of the few systematic attempts made by a secondary school to involve parents at a more than superficial level. In a similar vein, while acting as evaluation officer to the Community Education Development Centre (CEDC) in Coventry, I was responsible for recording several projects with a home–school emphasis, broadening into a community approach. These projects took me to many parts of Britain, where I was fortunate to meet teachers, other professionals and many parents in 'disadvantaged' areas: Salford, Leicester, Loughborough, Blackburn, London, Bradford and Batley (see Chapter 9). An especially valuable job – valuable to me, that is – was to visit and evaluate the work of the North Hull Neighbourhood Centre (see Chapter 10). I made a series of enjoyable forays to the North-east and was most courteously entertained, although the father in the house where I stayed had not been in full-time work for four years. This was one place where some genuine progress had been made towards parental participation and where the school had truly stimulated a community response.

I have also had opportunities to conduct evaluations in a wider community context. The Sports Council commissioned a study of its Action Sport programme in the West Midlands, which brought me into contact with some of the most optimistic, friendly and outgoing people I have met. There I was evaluating the community work of a boxer who not long before had been a leading contender for the middleweight championship of Britain. The visits for this project took me, physically and psychologically, into parts that I had never previously reached, although I have lived in the West Midlands for a long time. I oversaw an action–research project based in Coventry and Birkenhead, jointly funded by the Manpower Services Commission and a local charity, concerning the experiences, attitudes and aspirations of unemployed young women.[5] I made visits to a biscuit factory to try to involve workers in a shop floor university.

Over the years I have worked with numerous local authorities and charitable organisations, and I have had privileged access to many experiments conducted into the education of 'disadvantaged' pupils. I witnessed at close quarters (its Manchester headquarters was opposite one of the polytechnic buildings) the rise and fall of the Educational Disadvantage Unit, and was for a time a member of the language committee of the Assessment of Performance Unit.

'After such knowledge, what forgiveness?' T. S. Eliot asks. There have been many conferences on the subject of 'educational disadvantage' since the EPA Project, and I attended most of them, as either delegate or contributor, hearing speakers of unimpeachable integrity describe their work. Somehow the speeches did not sound right, though some were more authentic than others. It began to strike home that, despite plenty of effort, the problems continued to recur. The poor are still poor; the rich show no sign of handing over their disproportionate share of wealth; pupils from disadvantaged groups continue to fail at school, and despite the race relations industry, harmony does not prevail. Seen from the ground, however, the situation seems more hopeful. There are programmes, comparatively untried, that provide models for further action, and such models form the core of this book. My Manchester Polytechnic colleagues and I experimented with dialogue about relationships between home–school teachers and members of school staffs. It is through examining, and modifying, our own mode of presenting programmes to the people we want to help that we can hope to make progress. At one conference I organised in Manchester I asked some of the 'disadvantaged' women to come along and speak if they wished to – which a number of them did. They expressed amusement at some of the solemnities they heard, and then moved to another conceptual level as they reflected on their experience. They considered the views of the project workers, looked the evaluators in the eye, said what they thought about the ghastly flats they lived in and talked about their aspirations for their children and themselves.

The more often we can be face-to-face with our clients, the better the hope for dialogue. I organised a 'happening' when I brought administrators, home–school teachers and parent governors together at a Liverpool conference, but I have had personal experience of few others when clients were present as equals at an educational conference. Indeed, at one such, organised by the International Community Education Association in Dublin, a group of unemployed young men and women presented themselves but were forced to resort to busking outside the dining room in order to draw attention to their cause; few delegates seemed interested. This was just one more example of the continued prevalence of an authoritarian and paternalistic attitude towards 'disadvantaged' people, which makes them rightly resistant to and sometimes disdainful of the programmes set up to help them. These paternalistic attitudes found their fullest expression in the liberal theories and practice of 'compensatory education' in the 1960s.

Plan of the book

Chapter 2 places the various theoretical approaches to educational disadvantage in an historical perspective. There have been consistent and strenuous efforts made by professional teachers to reduce the effects of 'disadvantaged' home circumstances upon children's school performance in the period since the Education Act of 1944, and especially since the Plowden Report on primary schools (1967).[6] However, much of this work has been – and sometimes still is – undertaken in the spirit that schools should try to make up to the child for the 'cultural deprivation' he/she has previously encountered. Many schools have laboured mightily to build bridges between themselves and their parents, but always from the point of view of the professional teacher. To describe these activities I have adopted the term 'communications model'; this model is explained, and schools operating under these influences are analysed, in Chapters 3 and 4. Chapter 5 reviews the work of home–school liaison teachers, an heroic and largely unrecognised group who deserve better briefing, so that they can exercise their skills and enthusiasm to greater effect. Some lessons that can be drawn from all this effort are discussed in Chapter 6, where it is suggested first that co-operative effort is feasible, despite the many unfavourable events which continually suggest the contrary, and secondly that community education is therefore the best hope for a better future.

Part Two of the book records examples of whole educational systems, projects organised by local education authorities and charitable trusts that provide practical demonstrations of how to involve parents in a more significant way in educational decision-making. Chapter 7 reports findings from a study undertaken in Coventry, including some hard data to support the hypothesis that community education policies can produce dramatic improvements in educational attainment. Chapters 8 and 9 spell out practical details, with examples, for schools that would like to emulate these achievements through changes in their curriculum and organisation. Chapter 10 presents studies of neighbourhood centres that have involved parents of young children to the extent of giving them a measure of autonomy.

Part Three attempts to square up to the great issue of why, despite the impressive extension of educational opportunities since 1944, so many pupils take so little from the education system and what can be done about this. First, at the policy level, there are the disastrous failures of successive British governments to deliver what has been so frequently promised, compounded by the ideological shifts between political parties. Nigel Middleton astutely described the shaping of educational policy:

> the advance of public education is always haltered; when the Right are in power they supply restrictive facilities to meet the wishes of their supporters. When the Left are in power they have grandiose plans but fail to find the means of fulfilling them. Great expectations are raised which faced with the realities of government they cannot satisfy. When they lose momentum and falter, the more politically astute Right are ready to move in.[7]

Secondly, there has been the grave difficulty that the liberal policies were, as A. H. Halsey has put it, based on an inadequate theory of learning, which failed to note that 'for many pupils the major determinants of educational attainment' are 'not schoolmasters but social situations, not curriculum but motivation, not formal access to the school but support in the family and the community'.[8]

What perhaps follows from this analysis is that those who regard themselves as disadvantaged by the operation of the system should look to themselves to make good its deficiencies. The teaching profession can help the process by trying to achieve clarity about the purposes of popular education, and of parental participation; by intensifying the search for a more adequate learning theory; by becoming more outward looking and eager to co-operate with other caring agencies. The disadvantaged parents can aim to become more aware and more adept at competing for scarce educational resources. Both should start by rejecting all paternalistic prejudgements about intellectual capacities and ceilings, taking heart from the numerous examples of parent involvement and self-help groups recorded in Chapters 9 and 10.

The book draws examples of good practice from the widest possible range of educational establishments, including special schools.

I hope this will not give anyone the impression that I somehow regard the 'disadvantaged' as a single group or that I associate ethnic minorities with special treatment. Good practice is good practice, and lessons can be learned from sincere and intelligent efforts to implement educational experiments wherever they occur. The community education I advocate is blind to gender, age and to ethnic group, deaf to the sounds of stereotyping by IQ and other crude descriptive systems. It is concerned with identifying and finding appropriate learning responses to special learning needs whenever and wherever they occur.

CHAPTER 2

Historical perspective

In the 1960s the atmosphere in the British state educational service was optimistic. There was a strong and pervasive feeling that what went on in schools made a difference to pupils' life chances, even though this was in the context of what A. H. Halsey has called 'a class-ridden prosperity'.[1] Every school-leaver found a job as soon as he or she wanted; and 'good' non-selective schools could dedicate themselves to ensuring that their pupils were well prepared for the world of work, where it was clearly understood (as a headteacher once told me) that they would be 'followers' not 'leaders'. It seems, in retrospect, a time of almost primeval innocence.

For perhaps the only period in British educational history there was a widely accepted agreement that investment in the nation's children was reliable and productive. Higher education expanded vastly under the auspices of the Robbins Report (1963); and there were other high-quality government-sponsored reports making many common-sense and practical recommendations.[2] It was not known at the time that raising the school-leaving age to sixteen, first recommended by the Crowther Committee in 1959, would take such an unconscionable time (until 1972) to enact; nor that it would be 1979 before the vast majority (86 per cent) of maintained school pupils were in comprehensive schools.[3] The very fact that these weighty documents had been published and these liberal recommendations had been made produced a feeling that things were looking up in the education world. At least, no one could now deny the existence of the 'Newsom' pupils making up 'half our future' but receiving nothing like half the available resources.[4] Concrete proposals for equalising opportunities had been made and were on the political agenda, and there was a strong belief that improving the environment of learning would raise the level of achievement.

The 1960s were in general a good time for the environmentalists, vigorously led by J. McVicker Hunt and Benjamin Bloom in the USA. McVicker Hunt abandoned the notion of fixed intelligence and abilities, emphasising rather the power of a child's environment, and particularly the quality of mothering, on intellectual growth.[5] Bloom, in *Stability and Change in Human Characteristics*, assembled world-wide longitudinal research and reached a conclusion that deeply influenced US and British education policy for the next decade.[6] He reported that intellectual growth occurred most rapidly in the first four or five years of life, with variability in an individual's performance at its greatest in the early years. Hence the best time to enrich the environment and stimulate intellectual growth was in this period of rapid development, the pre-school years. This was one very significant theoretical base for the massive US Head Start programme, which was launched in the summer of 1965. Despite vastly over-inflated expectations – and, in retrospect, an amazing concentration on changes in something called IQ as the main measure of success – Head Start performed an important function in convincing Americans that they were truly conducting a 'war on poverty'.

The early evaluation of the Head Start programme, conducted by the Westinghouse Learning Corporation, concentrated almost entirely on cognition.[7] Its most widely publicised finding was that the cognitive gains made by children in the programme were often lost after children had been in elementary school for a few years. The first message that came across the Atlantic was that Head Start was a failure. Barbara Tizard accepted this account to the extent that she wrote in an influential monograph:

> In so far, then, as the expansion of early schooling is seen as a way of avoiding later school failure or of closing the social gap in achievement, we already know it to be doomed to failure. It would perhaps be sensible for research workers to point this out very clearly to public authorities at an early stage.[8]

Subsequent reports greatly modified this interpretation, especially one from Yale University in 1976, which found significant long-term effects as Head Start children went through school. The definitive book, by Zigler and Valentine, collates a vast array of facts about health and social care programmes.[9] It makes the point that the

pre-school can be regarded from two points of view, which Blank
solemnly called 'shared rearing pre-schools' and 'academic pre-
schools'.[10] They can be seen mainly as preparing children for schooling or as valuable extensions of the 'desire of women to have support
services in the rearing of their children'.[11] However, the notion of an
academic pre-school proved particularly alien to English nursery
schoolteachers.

The pre-school emphasis in Head Start, which transferred very
strongly to England and Wales through the Plowden Report (1967)
and the subsequent EPA Project, was a benign influence, in spite of
the ferocious controversies engendered by some of the materials and
methods. The message about 'shared rearing' was not received until
recently but it was there, and has gradually come to the surface.

A further theoretical input has proved anything but benign. It
arrived simultaneously from the psychologist McVicker Hunt and
the anthropologist Oscar Lewis, and strongly impressed itself upon
the collective consciousness of workers from many different disciplines. This is the idea of 'cultural deprivation' requiring 'compensatory education'. Lewis's studies of Latin American people achieved
paperback best-seller fame; *La Vida* is recommended to readers in the
British paperback edition as 'a picture of an entirely rootless society
without rules, without strings, without hierarchies'.[12] His term 'the
culture of poverty', whether or not an accurate account of the people
he studied, was carefully construed and persuasively presented.
Over seventy traits were identified. On the family level these
included the absence of childhood as a specially prolonged and pro-
tected stage in the life cycle, early initiation into sex, free unions, a
relatively high incidence of the abandonment of wives and children,
female- or mother-centred families, a strong predisposition to
authoritarianism, and lack of privacy. Other traits included weak
ego structure, strong present-time orientation with relatively little
ability to defer gratification, a widespread belief in male superiority
and a high tolerance for psychological pathology of all sorts.

Since these behaviours were displayed consistently enough for
them to be observed and categorised, however, the people must have
been conforming to custom or rules, contrary to what has been previously quoted. They were not rootless, since they competed for
familial attention.

Lewis's term degenerated into a slogan, and the slogan was
bowdlerised into 'culturally deprived' – a complete contradiction of

Lewis's position, since no one can be deprived of a culture (even one of poverty), particularly not those who have been *socialised into* a particular culture. McVicker Hunt added the notion that the poor were 'deprived' of certain key experiences, which put them at a competitive disadvantage compared to their more fortunate middle-class compatriots. The poor were 'incompetent', and enrichment programmes were necessary to make good these deficits.

The 'enrichment' programmes that followed were strongly paternalistic. They began with a statement of objectives derived from a list of 'deficits' that the child was known to possess because he or she came from a particular group in society. To those deficits already identified were added others concerned with the child's language. The more extreme authorities such as Bereiter and Engelmann concluded that the young disadvantaged were verbally destitute, bereft of language and requiring compensatory education programmes like those given to non-English speakers.[13] In Britain the influence of Bernstein was paramount; his early work confidently asserted that working-class children used a 'public language', consistently marked by limited vocabulary and poor syntax.[14] Bernstein drew up lists of these features, which were taught to teachers in initial and post-experience courses. As the theory developed, 'disadvantaged language', now identified with that of the lower working class, was called a 'restricted code' (as opposed to the 'elaborated code' used by the middle class): 'it is restricted in the sense that it can be used, for example, in the home or the gang, but it is not adequate or acceptable in other circumstances'. In contrast he calls advantaged language an 'elaborated code'. 'It is a language in which advanced thought is possible; it is sensitive and flexible': thus wrote Andrew Wilkinson in a text book widely used and highly regarded in teacher-training institutions.[15]

I do not at this stage wish to discuss language and other 'intervention' programmes in detail, but only to highlight the patronising tone that prevailed among educators (whatever their primary discipline); the insensitivity – despite their middle-class advantages – with which they approached their clients; the reinforcement of teachers' middle-class prejudices; the denigration of the language and mores of disadvantaged people, all apparently much the same whether living in the USA, Puerto Rico or Britain; the conceptual crudity and confusion. (In addition to the psychologists and sociologists, there were also the specialists in learning difficulties, who were invited to

conferences on the grounds that the socio-economically disadvantaged were synonymous with the mentally retarded.)

If the 1960s were a time of optimism, the theoretical bases and
attitudes upon which the intervention programmes were based were
fatally flawed. Compensatory education compounded the communication difficulties inherent in any public education system by
defining pupils and parents as inherently inferior, deficient, incompetent. The professionals do not of course intend to convey such a
message, but any kind of programme administered on behalf of
others and for the benefit of others is in danger of being interpreted
in this way and rejected either overtly – as when the people of St
Paul's, Bristol, refused to accept a community centre offered to them
– or covertly, by withdrawing mentally.

The EPA Project (1969–72) did not altogether escape this trap, but
it placed better home–school relationships at the centre of its
activities and was much less fixated on the question of IQ gains.
Operating in four areas in England and Wales, and also in Scotland,
it generated enormous publicity and reached optimistic conclusions
about the potential of pre-schooling and of the idea of the community primary school – see Figure 2.1. Despite inevitable reconsidera-
tions and re-evaluations of the concept of Educational Priority
Areas, 'many of the current ideas for overcoming disadvantage still
have their origin in the work done on the EPA projects – notably on
the community school, the need for flexibility in curriculum and
organisation, the importance of pre-schooling and the need for local
diagnosis'.[16]

Figure 2.1 The main recommendations of the Halsey Report
(1972)
- *Pre-schooling* was the outstandingly economical and effective
  way of applying the principle of positive discrimination and of
  raising educational standards in Educational Priority Areas.
- The idea of the *community school* was shown to have great sub-
  stance and powerful implications for community regeneration.
- There are practical ways of improving the partnership between
  families and *schools* in *Educational Priority Areas*.
- There are practical ways of improving the *quality of learning* in
  EPA schools.

Historically, then, much present-day educational activity can be traced to the 1960s. The movement has survived the widespread doubts raised about the effectiveness of schooling;[17] and the present book is testimony to the continued, if muted, support given to its ideas by local education authorities, and to the notion of action research, which was also given renewed currency by the Halsey EPA Project. What has perhaps survived best into the 1980s is a strong belief in the activity of involving parents, without too much emphasis on enquiring about its efficacy. This may be called the 'communications' approach, and it is a considerable step forward from the 'compensatory' model. It supposes that work which is optimistic, which takes place in a friendly and cheery atmosphere, and which attracts parents into schools, or sends staff into homes for any reason, is good in itself. Such beliefs have been firmly held since at least 1968, when Young and McGeeney proposed their 'syllogism of parental participation':

> A rise in the level of parental encouragement augments their children's performance at school.
> Teachers, by involving parents in the school, bring about a rise in the level of parental encouragement.
> Therefore, teachers, by involving parents in the school, augment the children's performance.[18]

It is necessary to bear both traditions – 'compensatory' and 'communications' – in mind when attempting a perspective on the present state of parental involvement. The latter approach has operated outside the 'deficit' model, and much of the work reported in this book derives from it. The Halsey project also operated within the spirit of this model, but could not altogether escape the *Zeitgeist* of the 1960s. In following up the idea of 'positive discrimination' for deprived areas, DES Circular 11/67 declared unequivocally:

> The Government believe that better educational provision can, by compensating for the effects of social deprivation and the depressing physical environment in which many children grow up, make an important contribution to overcoming family poverty.

The better face of the compensatory model comprises those documents representing problem-orientated thinking, of which a good example was that prepared for the City of Leicester in 1979. It moved from an identification of the problem to an immediate statement of the action to be taken:

Low morale, lack of influence over and a sense of alienation from the public authorities will be tackled through community development, better communications and improved facilities for the unorganised. Community development will be achieved in a variety of ways including the creation of residents' associations in Housing Action Areas, the support of community organisations by neighbourhood development officers working from neighbourhood centres which will be provided as a focus for community activity, and the support of voluntary and self-help projects, whether they be the provision of needed facilities or activities. Better communications between residents and authorities and amongst residents will improve understanding and confidence. Several projects from main programme and urban programme will seek to improve communications including pump-priming assistance to community newspapers.[19]

There is nothing intrinsically wrong with the procedure of documenting disadvantages; they certainly exist, and the families who use the schools have to overcome physical and emotional problems directly generated by the environment in which they live. What so much concerns critics of this approach is that socio-cultural factors soon become *explanations* of educational failure. The symptoms are taken for the cause. Poor performance is accounted for by factors external to the schooling system, by the extra-educational attributes of the child. The victims are blamed for the difficulties that overwhelm them. Instead of considering possible malfunctions in the education system, teachers and administrators look for explanations in terms of 'cultural deprivation' or 'deficits'. Sharp and Green wrote of one teacher in their study school on a large working-class housing estate:

Mrs X sees her pupils as the products of largely unstable and uncultured backgrounds, with parents who are in various combinations irresponsible, incompetent, illiterate, 'clueless', uninterested and unappreciative of education, and who as a result fail to prepare their children adequately for the experiences they will be offered in school. The parents, especially the mothers, tend to be spoken of very disparagingly. The mothers are perceived as generally immature and unable to cope, having too many young children either by accident or design whilst they are still too young. The teacher declares that many mothers go to work to help pay off rent arrears and electricity bills incurred through bad management. She castigates them for creating latchkey children and for frittering away their conscience money on toys and unsuitable clothes (hot pants, etc.) in an attempt to relieve 'their guilt' at neglecting them.[20]

Similar prejudice is uncovered in the Swann Report (1985), which attributes much of the school failure of young Afro-Caribbeans 'to prejudice and discrimination bearing directly on children within the educational system, as well as outside it'.[21]

A communications model has many of the attributes of the Plowden Report's 'partnership' or Douglas's 'co-operation',[22] castigated by Sharp because 'the sort of partnership envisaged really amounts to parents helping teachers to achieve goals specified by teachers in ways specified by teachers'.[23] Goode uses the communications model to 'represent increased parent–teacher contact and parental involvement in schools as a way of informing parents in a non–problematic way about school life and their supportive role in it.'[24] Even the communications level of involvement is apparently rare in British schools, however. In secondary schools, as HMI noted in 1984:

> Very few of the schools attempted to enlist the help of parents directly in curriculum matters, but readily called on them to join forces in eradicating undesirable behaviour or attitudes which adversely affected work. Even in one school, which in general had excellent relationships with parents, written communications acquainting them of the school's concern often carried an impression that it was the parents' responsibility to find a solution, and must have conveyed in some of them a sense of being accused.[25]

The level of parental involvement that would make a genuine difference to the delivery of an educational service to disadvantaged pupils may be called the 'participatory' model. It is a world away from notions of compensation and is a transformation of the communications or 'busy-work' approach. Parents are viewed within the participatory model as people exercising some control over their own lives, with more than marginal responsibility for the development and education of their children. They are seen as capable of personal self-development, initiating, organising and sustaining activities. The very thought of these people being verbally destitute is enough to reduce one to helpless laughter, in view of their linguistic vigour and inventiveness. It would be possible to produce a list of traits common to people I have observed in Manchester, Hull, Coventry and Birkenhead which in every way contradicts that suggested by Oscar Lewis (though not necessarily invalidating his account of the population he studied).

To say that there are a few examples of home–school co-operation is not to suggest that the burden of the compensatory model has been, or shows much sign of being, lifted. However, cautious experiments in reducing educational disadvantage, whatever their limitations, have been sufficiently widespread to justify one in asking why they have not been universally adopted. The next chapter describes and analyses the procedures of an outstanding primary school, operating within the philosophy and traditions of the communications model.

CHAPTER 3

The communications model: an inner-city multicultural primary school

It is hard to sustain the belief in the inevitability of 'progress' that was so marked a feature of those Victorian values to which we are sometimes exhorted to return. In education, especially as regards disadvantaged pupils, some things have certainly become worse in Britain over recent years. Schools are increasingly dependent on parental support, not for activities that will add to the child's educational experience, but in order to sustain it at the basic level of providing books and buildings. Inspiriting out-of-school activities, such as those at the primary school described below, have been deeply affected by the long industrial dispute of 1985–6. In these circumstances, any experiments in linking home and school that have been observed at close quarters may be of some significance when a climate is re-established which permits schools to look beyond the necessities of daily survival.

Hamm Green School

Hamm Green Primary School in Manchester consisted of approximately 250 children and twelve teaching staff, plus the headmaster and the school secretary. Of the children, roughly 32 per cent were of Caribbean origin, 28 per cent of Asian origin and 40 per cent

indigenous 'whites'. The latter group was by no means homogeneous, including, among others, children of Polish and Chilean origin.
The proportion of one ethnic group to another was changing in the
school; in the upper years there was a greater percentage of West
Indians than in the lower school, which was becoming increasingly
Asian. Classed as EPA, the school was set in pleasant, leafy sur-
roundings and stood on the edge of the inner city, receiving children
both from there and from older suburbs with more trees and gar-
dens.

Physically the school was attractive both inside and out. On the
door of the main entrance was a sign welcoming visitors. Friends of
teachers came in to help, student teachers came on visits and practices, 'ethnic' dance teachers visited, policmen on public-relations
duty were seen from time to time, an ITV camera crew filmed the
school's big band, and staff and children were interviewed on local
radio. In many ways it was a showpiece: an 'active multiracial
school'. The children also went on numerous visits outside school:
the Athenaeum Theatre, the Science Museum, limestone caves in
Derbyshire, an outdoor pursuits centre and the local art gallery, to
name but a few. The children were used to meeting outsiders, to
receiving and talking to them. Parents were always warmly welcomed. They had at least three opportunities a year to attend shows,
and were invited to two parents' evenings.

The head had a very outgoing approach, promoting the name of
the school whenever possible, in terms of its atmosphere rather than
its 'success'. He claimed only that there was no gloom at Hamm
Green, and that expectations of *all* pupils were high. He pointed with
enthusiasm to the achievements of his school, signs of which were
placed near and around his office. Immediately behind his desk was
the schools' chess trophy. On a small table at the entrance to his
office was an album containing photographs of school events: outings, open days, shows, important visitors, and the like.

The main thrust of the headmaster's energy was felt in the school's
musical activities. He had set up a big band, arranged music for it,
conducted and accompanied it, usually on piano and sometimes on
trumpet. He practised with the band during lunch-times, after
school, and on Wednesday afternoons. Three other teachers were
also involved in the band playing different instruments, one the flute
and two clarinets. The nature of these musical activities changed
slightly in the course of the year. In the autumn term, when principal

members of the previous year's big band had gone on to secondary school, there was a school orchestra consisting of the brass players who were left and children playing recorders, flutes, guitars and the xylophone, while new brass players were prepared. By the end of the Easter term, musical activity included this orchestra, a junior orchestra, a growing big band and a choir. By the summer term the big band took over, though sometimes the junior orchestra carried on and performed in the summer show. The school also put on a Christmas show, a 'cabaret' for guests of the school to raise money for the music fund, a show at the end of the summer, and numerous outings to perform at other schools. The children put on a special show for old age pensioners at Christmas and in the summer.

The head was quick to praise a good performance by the whole band or a particular section. He always told audiences at shows about the members of the band and the instruments they played, and often asked a child to stand up and be noticed. He could also be critical of the band's performance, and was open in pointing out mistakes – using gentle humour, which often worked wonders in sustaining effort, without diminishing self-esteem. He encouraged activities that enriched the children's lives, and in choosing his staff looked for people with an extra-curricular interest to offer. One teacher took a gymnastics class, another organised the school's chess club and took a team to tournaments, others ran pottery classes and the folk dance club. All these activities took place after school hours and were enthusiastically attended, so that the children had a range of contexts in which they could discover their talents; they were encouraged to be constructive, to do things for pleasure and self-development.

Turning the school round

The school had not always been in such cheerful circumstances. Indeed, when this head took up his post, discipline was poor, with children refusing to co-operate in lessons, and low levels of literacy prevailing. He and the deputy head devised a twin-pronged strategy, on the one hand developing the centres of interest described above, on the other tackling the literacy problem through a programme called Three Pages a Day, using the good old Wide Range Readers of Fred and Eleanor Schonell.[1] Every child from the first to fourth year read aloud three pages a day in addition to class reading practice.

To make this possible, each class was split into Readers and Listeners, the latter being children with reading ages above their chronological age. Thus was the monitorial system reborn!

By the time they reached the fourth year, the children were reading nine pages a day, and literacy levels had risen dramatically since the crisis period. Merit schemes were also started about this time; positive behaviours were reinforced in a wide variety of ways ranging from the formal to the very informal and personal. On the formal level the school was divided into four houses, which competed for a league championship. Points were given for good work, for answering promptly in class, for achievement in quick tests and for succeeding in basic responsibilities such as keeping one's own school equipment together and handing work in on time. There was also a merit badge system. Each term a head boy and girl were nominated, a number of prefects were named, and jobs were allocated to various children. On the whole, these jobs were popular, and to be given one was considered a favour or reward. A list of these post-holders was put up on the 'official' notice-board in the concourse.

Inclusion or exclusion from the main activities of the school was used as a sanction. Children could play in the orchestra, sing in the choir and take part in the plays only if they showed themselves co-operative and reliable. Children taking part in these activities but who disrupted them would no longer be allowed to participate, and re-acceptance would be difficult. On the other hand, diffident children who wanted to take part were gradually drawn in. Children were not taken on school outings unless they showed themselves to be reliable in school. The hidden sanction was that such behaviour might disturb the pleasant atmosphere. The school was indeed a very cheerful place, the head having a good sense of humour, which the children appreciated. Humour also characterised the deputy head and a number of other staff.

Nine of the twelve members of staff had been at the school for six years or more. They usually acted as a unit in presenting the school's policies to children and parents, and this was a great source of strength. There were nevertheless two camps, one based round the deputy head, which was basically in agreement about the kind of school they wanted, what they regarded as educationally desirable and the atmosphere in which this should be achieved. Members of this group regularly attended courses and conferences on education in a multicultural school, as well as having active personal and social lives. The teachers outside this group by no means constituted a homogeneous unit; among them, however, were three teachers of whom the deputy head was critical. She felt that these teachers, two in particular, had a very different image of the school they would like. Both sent the children out to play and locked their rooms; one caused a school crisis when she hit a child and the parent complained. Both these features – locking away one's possessions, and physically punishing – were contrary to the ethos of the school, which was to encourage children to be responsible and to discourage negative behaviour by showing the *social consequences* of a refusal to co-operate. The school aimed to make work and co-operation with the school a pleasurable activity to be worked towards. Positive reinforcement was used by the head and deputy, whereas these two teachers were seen as using negative reinforcement to bring about desired behaviour.

Despite these disagreements, support was provided by senior staff when teachers ran into difficulties.

Factors in success

Features of the organisation of Hamm Green, the teaching methods employed and attitudes implicit in these methods can be identified as accounting, at least in part, for the success of the school.

High expectations

- In activities, notably in orchestra and gym for concerts and performances.
- In work, indicated in the display of large amounts of children's work.
- In behaviour: children were not expected to misbehave; disappointment and surprise were expressed when they did so.

Consistency

Teachers' expectations of pupils' behaviour were consistent across the school and through time:

- In incentives and sanctions: good work/behaviour was praised and rewarded with full inclusion in the school's activities; poor work/behaviour was answered with exclusion from some activities, and with displeasure;
- In what was valued and what was devalued: staff co-operated in conveying a more or less uniform set of values;
- In the teaching of each particular teacher: work on the wall reflected, in more pragmatic terms, what the children had studied; for example, only cursive script would be used on the board, which reinforced the learning of this handwriting skill; the children were expected to transfer the learning from one situation to another, and what was expected was made explicit.

Continuity

- Behaviour modification was conducted over a long period. Children knew they were being observed all the time by all the teachers. They knew that present behaviour would affect future treatment.
- There was continuity between home and school. Parents attended school functions, came in when a child 'seriously misbehaved' and were mentioned by teachers, as were siblings. The children also had homework twice a week, which was signed by the parents.

Openness towards errors and failings

It was explicitly pointed out by one teacher that most of the West Indian children she taught were evangelical Christians and placed great emphasis on honesty and frankness. This may have predisposed the children to respond favourably when they were treated with directness.

Structure

- Clarity of expectations.
- Emphasis on procedure, setting out.
- A lot of support.

- Clear constraints on behaviour.
- A strong emphasis on reading and writing sustained through the whole school, with progress monitored on record cards.

Humorous and caring environment

- The children were relaxed by the constant humour of the head and deputy, and were put in a position to feel equal, to banter good-humouredly.
- 'Care' was shown by knowing about family troubles and showing concern over them, by caring for the children when they were troubled and sick, by spending time on extra-curricula activities and by taking the children on outings and courses.

Resourcefulness

In offering a variety of fields in which children with different tendencies could participate and excel, e.g. the big band, gymnastics, chess, folk dancing.

A multicultural school?

The organisation of the school took little account of its being a multicultural community. The purpose was to raise the self-esteem of all the children and to integrate them through the use of symbols and rituals. There was not much provision for ethnic minorities in the choice of reading materials, and there was no explicit focus on black culture. Rather, the emphasis was on treating every person as an equal and valid representative of the human race, which received one expression through public displays such as a frieze of 'new faces' in the autumn term. These faces varied from pure white to deep brown. Lips, virtually all of them smiling, were of every shape and size; hair was black and curly, black and straight, brown and wavy, blond(e) and straight, red and fuzzy. It was felt that this display indicated acceptance by the school of its multiracial population, as did the four panels in the hall depicting school activities. Here the teacher was represented standing by the vaulting-horse, which a black boy was jumping; a white boy was doing a handstand, a black girl a cartwheel.

This rather touching belief in the power of symbolic representation has, of course, been extended to television, where a token black is to be found in most soap operas and police series, performing functions rarely, if ever, seen in real life. So the children may be doing gymnastics together, and it is true that they are all treated in exactly the same way during their school hours. But nobody now needs reminding that racial discrimination exists outside the school, or that young blacks and Asians resent it. Nothing will be accomplished by pretending that children are unaware of ethnic differences, or that British society is uniquely tolerant and will in due course 'assimilate' all these different groups without rancour. Far better, one might feel, to acknowledge the realities of the multiracial society, that has come into existence, and to begin the process of helping our pupils adjust to what exists.

The Hamm Green staff has developed strategies for coping with a potentially dangerous situation. They succeeded in containing their problems but, one suspects, at the cost of not resisting the development of difficulties elsewhere. The parents seemed well pleased with the tone of the school, and content with their rolf as supporters of a system over which they exercised no control and of a curriculum that varied according to the dictates and enthusiasms of those in charge. Hamm Green was, in fact, a good example of the communications model as defined in Chapter 2. The communication referred to is all in one direction: informing parents about what is going on, anticipating their approval and support. Thus, for all the friendliness and good humour of such a school, the buzz of communication had the end result of keeping parents at arms length. The professionals barely conceived of the idea that parents could have any contribution to make in their own right, and there was no thought of their becoming involved in decision-making. All may not be as well as it appears. Nobody 'in authority' listens, so important messages are not picked up. 'Riots', said Martin Luther King, 'are the language of the unheard'. Putting on a mask of well-being serves very well in the short run, and suits the purposes of the professionals who have to account for the conduct of their institution. But ethnic minority parents start Saturday classes to provide the education they feel is lacking in state schools.

This blithe expectation that parents will always be quiet supporters was the source of some rude shocks to staff in the next school to be studied.

CHAPTER 4

The communications model: group work in a day special school

The Downton Park project

I was asked to evaluate and report on a long-running project at Downton Park Day Special School in Manchester, during which strenuous efforts were made to improve contacts between the school and homes and to persuade parents to join discussion groups with other parents.[1] The hope was that they would identify common problems and through contacts with one another, under the guidance of professional group workers, restructure these problems and increase their control over their own lives. There would be benefits to the school and to the children in the form of more positive support, and to the parents themselves.

Though the project lasted seven years and was supported throughout by funds from a charitable trust, few of its original aims were fully realised. There was an abundance of goodwill and a strong resolve to sustain the project's activities, despite numerous changes in its personnel and a massive reorganisation within the charitable trust itself. A consequence of this longevity was that unsuccessful approaches could be abandoned or modified and replaced by others more suited to the needs of the situation. A great deal was learned about the processes of communication between parents, teachers and social workers, about the skills necessary for effective group work and those required in order to sustain an innovatory educational project. But the hopes and expectations of the headteacher and staff of the school began to be fulfilled only in the final two years of the project. This lack of progress was due, in part, to the emergence of a group of parents whose own aspirations and expectations proved to be quite different from those of the professionals, and to widely differing perspectives among the teachers, social workers, voluntary association staff, sociologists and psychologists who became involved over the years.

The project began by asking: what are the needs of parents and children in the inner-city catchment area of a special school? Having identified some of these needs through a series of systematic visits to homes, the project team had to decide on a course of action. It found the threshold of the home relatively easy to cross, but in the reverse direction the school threshold was another matter. Parents stopped there; they did not cross, and in general they did not even approach. There were many difficulties – for example, the complex transport system of the inner-city, since the school's catchment area was wide – but there was nevertheless little evidence that parents were more involved when their children attended mainstream schools closer to home. How, then, to initiate a dialogue, to bring parents into meaningful contact with teachers? The consequence of giving these parents a genuine opportunity to comment on the education their children were receiving was not properly considered beforehand.

In answer to the question of what the needs of the parents and children were, two points of view were represented. The social scientist whose report on the needs survey was published at an early stage held that 'Group work is aimed at the long-term alleviation of family and social problems through the active participation of parents themselves'.[2] The approach of the headteacher had an entirely different emphasis, as the following statement by him shows:

> If parents can be brought together in groups and salutary relationships formed, the members of the group may learn to see many of their problems as capable of solution. Clearly, whoever is appointed should be an expert in his field. He must be able to advise and help any other group leaders on matters affecting their groups, and have some understanding of subnormality.[2]

Of these two viewpoints in the first instance the published report proved the more influential, as the group workers turned to it for guidance.

Parental meetings

It was, in the circumstances, a bold course of action that the project decided to adopt. Parents would be invited to form groups and to hold meetings in the school, under the general direction of a full-time community worker. Transport would be provided. Discussion would be free and untrammelled, with topics generated from within the group itself. The teachers hoped that the process of discussion would produce a supportive band of parents, eager to improve the quality of their own and their children's education. Instead, what came into being that first term was a series of meetings in which parents expressed distrust of, and aggression towards, the school. They believed there was not enough academic study in the school, that there were too many craft subjects and extra-curricular activities, insufficient homework, outdated and inadequate books. They felt that attendance at the school caused a stigma. The activities of the group, far from soothing the staff of the school and supplementing its work, were seen by them as a threat. Differences began to be noticeable between the perspectives of the community worker and those of the teachers.

The outcome of this first venture can in retrospect be seen as inevitable. Hunt specifically stated that one of the purposes of bringing parents together was 'consciousness-raising', leading to 'a change in social expectations about one's role and place in society'.[4] The person appointed for the role was a community development officer who lived in a flat on the council estate and who had already committed himself to supporting self-help groups – which led to some conflict with the local authority about housing and the lack of amenities. It was not surprising that the first parental group organised by this community worker was, in his own words, 'filled with a certain amount of aggression – particularly by two sets of parents – towards the school'. Such meetings, at which 'everyone talked and no one listened', could have served a useful purpose. The guilt or shame that many parents felt was at first projected on to the school and later gave way to expressions of deep-rooted anxiety about their children's problems and how they as parents could contribute to tackling these problems in the home. This group, which regularly numbered about ten parents, went on to meet for twelve weekly sessions before having a break. Undoubtedly, it offered something substantial to some parents, but the teachers saw it differently:

> Certain members of staff felt angry and worried about group meetings; they felt parents were criticising things they did not fully understand and they saw the group worker as intruding into the affairs of the school and home–school relationships.[5]

The group worker by now seemed to see his role primarily in terms of a confrontation between parents and staff. A consultant psychologist was called in, but it was not clear to whom either he or the group worker was to be responsible. After failing to keep several important appointments, this group worker left to take up another post. His successor felt that he had inherited bad feeling on the part of both staff and parents.

It is by no means easy to decide whether these parental groups were 'successful' or not. Under the terms of reference given in Hunt they clearly succeeded in bringing parents together and in generating discussion of their problems.[6] In terms of the improvement of home–school relationships, they obviously failed disastrously. No provision was made for utilising the energy generated by the groups. No provision was made for the full discussions necessary if project staff and school staff were to reach a mutual understanding of what was meant by group work. This was fully apparent to an observer from the voluntary association:

> Group work itself is an experiment and has much to do to prove its worth. Why should teachers readily accept its methods, when on an individual basis parent–teacher discussion does take place, and when the results of the formation of a parent group can lead to friction and criticisms of teaching methods made by non-professionals?[7]

There was a short interim period between the two group workers, during which a Community Service Volunteers worker made a valuable contribution. The new social worker then produced a policy document 'to present my view of what the project is all about'. He called for 'an effective policy-making committee'. He stated his intention to concentrate on parents' discussion groups and began to visit homes. He found a problem in conceptualising for parents what the groups were and what their purpose was; when he attempted to establish evening groups, they survived for only three meetings. The social worker felt he must maintain an attitude of neutrality, although he was initially inclined to the view that if there were any bias it must be towards the parent. The headteacher commented that 'such an attitude, though understandable, began to dissipate the goodwill which awaited him'. However, the social worker did not perceive any initial goodwill and expressed feelings of discomfort and loneliness.

The project did somehow continue to operate, and both parties produced proposals that enabled a fresh start to be made. The head continued to make suggestions for development such as an afternoon group to run at the school (not on 'neutral ground', as the social worker wished). The social worker produced a paper criticising the way the project had been visualised and outlining different approaches to the one he had originally intended to develop – which he now believed was too narrow. Above all, he felt that such proposals should be discussed with the school staff, and this was finally achieved (after the project had been operating for three years). This was mainly an information-giving session, with comparatively little feedback from the staff, but it proved to be a useful exercise in improving relationships, supplemented by personal contact on an individual basis in the following weeks.

There was a shift in attitude by both parties that enabled the social worker to operate within the school without the sacrifice of his professional position. This was important to him; and its importance needs to be appreciated by the headteacher and staff of any school that seeks to involve social workers. On the other hand, the social worker never came to feel that he could accept the responsibility of crisis intervention; he was not a trained caseworker and, in his own view, not professionally competent to deal with such delicate situations.

Important lessons may be learned from this aspect of the project:

(1) There are many different social-worker perspectives, recognised and unrecognised.
(2) There are wide differences in perspective between teachers and social workers, recognised and unrecognised.
(3) The importance of careful presentation of personnel to one another can hardly be exaggerated; provision should be made for resolving conflicting points of view and also, although this is very difficult, for utilising the energy generated through the expression of legitimate differences of opinion on fundamental educational and social issues.

(4) On the question of parental representation, the social worker's perspective was more positive than that of the teachers.

Parental involvement in group work

Approaches

Over the period of the project, four main approaches to group work were tried:

(1) Unstructured, community-orientated. This produced a polarised, rather negative group of parents, dominated by a few couples and critical of the school; nevertheless the meetings continued for several terms and clearly fulfilled some parents' needs.
(2) Unstructured, 'social therapy' groups for parents. These took over many of the aspects of the previously mentioned group; attendance fell and the group closed; some vague fund-raising activities were undertaken.
(3) Structured evening groups, based on invited speakers; some good sessions were held, but attendance fell away.
(4) Semi-structured school-based afternoon groups for parents. These were the most successful ventures undertaken by the project; attention was paid to the need for some kind of structure. The best attended and most stimulating were those connected with the assessment unit, which automatically introduced new parents (all mothers) and generated its own school-based group dynamic.

Conclusions

- Group work can be undertaken in a special school, given sufficient determination and support by way of transport, etc.
- Group work is most likely to be productive when the group is centred upon topics of mutual interest, particularly the children's performance at school.
- The group worker must provide some kind of structure, as illustrated above. Overt 'social therapy' is often counter-productive, on the evidence available from this project; it seems to occur best when the group is functioning effectively round other foci.

- The group leader requires skills in relating to parents, to teachers, to the governing body and to the headteacher; this is a range of expertise unlikely to be found at the level of appointment possible – even if possessed by anyone. Much more careful guidance needs to be given to the group worker, so that role conflict is reduced to a minimum. A prior condition for offering a firmer brief to the group worker is the resolution of differences between parties on the managing body.

- Relatively few teachers became involved in the afternoon parents' groups; but of those who did, several made outstanding contributions. The most effective group was that connected with the assessment unit. The teacher in charge of the unit obviously enjoyed close relationships with the parents, and topics for conversation arose naturally and easily around the children and the videotapes that were used. More work of this kind could be encouraged; the group worker's contribution was very important in setting the tone of the meetings and keeping contact with the parents and could then be defined as focused on the school and facilitating more groups of this kind based on other classes. A firm commitment to such a programme, elicited from a majority of the school staff, would provide a proper foundation for progress towards genuine participation by parents.

CHAPTER 5

Joys and sorrows of Home–school liaison work

Muddle in the 1970s

The diversity of activities expected of a home–school liaison teacher (HSLT) or worker in a primary school in the 1970s can be deduced from Figure 5.1. It is impossible for any one person to respond adequately to all these demands. Yet it has been very common practice for an HSLT to be shared by more than one school. There could perhaps have been some excuse for this kind of miscalculation in 1974, when Cleveland LEA appointed ten HSLTs to nine infant, nine junior and two secondary schools, under an Urban Aid Grant; but the same kind of appointments were still being made in 1985. When do we start to move forward?

The aims of the Cleveland Project were to build links between home and school and to try to bring parents to a realisation of the importance of their role in the education of their children.[1] The HSLT was part of the school staff, with teaching commitments, and much of the work was therefore done after hours. The tasks could include pre-school visits (which familiarise parents and children with someone in the school and encourage the use of toy libraries, etc.), getting parents involved in school activities (some parents worked in the classroom, and teachers made use of their particular skills), the setting up of parents' rooms and mother-and-toddler groups, visiting the homes of children with learning difficulties as a result of illness or family problems, giving support to parents whose children had been referred to educational guidance, personal contact with

Figure 5.1 A home–school liaison teache

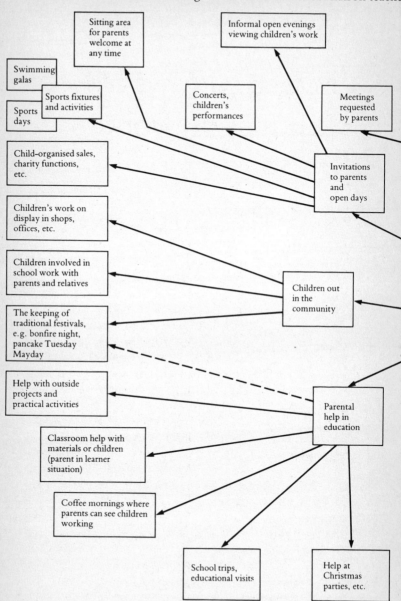

Adapted from: Broome, R. (1977), *Parental Involvement Schemes*

:ivities: the communications model

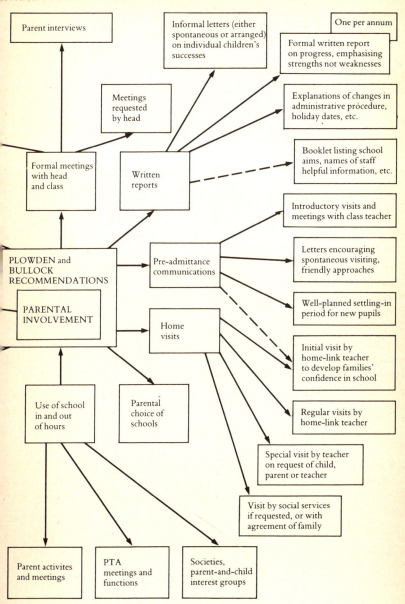

Parent interviews

Informal letters (either spontaneous or arranged) on individual children's successes

One per annum

Formal written report on progress, emphasising strengths not weaknesses

Meetings requested by head

Explanations of changes in administrative procedure, holiday dates, etc.

Formal meetings with head and class

Written reports

Booklet listing school aims, names of staff helpful information, etc.

Introductory visits and meetings with class teacher

PLOWDEN and BULLOCK RECOMMENDATIONS

Pre-admittance communications

Letters encouraging spontaneous visiting, friendly approaches

PARENTAL INVOLVEMENT

Well-planned settling-in period for new pupils

Home visits

Initial visit by home-link teacher to develop families' confidence in school

Use of school in and out of hours

Parental choice of schools

Regular visits by home-link teacher

Special visit by teacher on request of child, parent or teacher

Visit by social services if requested, or with agreement of family

Parent activites and meetings

PTA meetings and functions

Societies, parent-and-child interest groups

lake, P. *Remedial Education Programmes and Progress.* Longman.

new pupils and their parents, and involvement with youth and community groups.

The HSLTs involved in the project found that parents became more educationally aware; misunderstandings on all sides had been avoided by the close parental contact, and class teachers had been helped to understand each child's background. Some of the difficulties arising from the nature of the job were an overlap with outside agencies, and the danger that the teacher could become burdened with too many social problems not within his or her brief or time. In one area where the HSLTs were attached to four schools they felt that the area was too large and it was difficult to get to know colleagues and parents. They had been doing remedial work although they emphasised that the HSLTs job must not be confused with that of the remedial teacher. It was felt that in-service training would be useful before an appointment was taken up, and an essential point was for the HSLTs to be fully aware of all outside agencies and the services they offer, and to use them whenever necessary. An awareness of child development and pre-learning activities was also important.

Most HSLTs were shared by two schools; five of them were shared by four. 'Although this curtails the amount of attention each family can receive it ensures links and continuity, which are particularly valuable in the infant and junior schools, and is also more of a viable financial proposition to an LEA than one HSLT to a school.'[2]

By 1977 the Urban Aid Grant had spawned ill-conceived, school-centred projects all over England and Wales.

Confusion in the 1980s

Much excellent work, it goes without saying, has been accomplished; but by 1985 there were few signs of any focusing down to manageable aims and objectives. The job description for HSLTs in Lancashire, for example, encompassed the following responsibilities:[3]

(1) To facilitate communications between school, the educational service and the homes of the pupils.
(2) To foster better understanding between teachers and parents, teachers and children, children and children, about the different customs, religious beliefs and culture.

(3) To encourage a partnership between teachers and parents in the education of the child.

(4) To help in the development of a corporate school community.

(5) To become completely familiar with the school's philosophy and practices.

(6) To visit the homes of the children in order to:
    (a) help create a friendly and supportive atmosphere;
    (b) explain school policy and organisation as the need arises;
    (c) encourage good attendance and punctuality;
    (d) make contact before the children's admission with a view to encouraging mothers and children to visit the school to familiarise themselves with the practice and organisation.

(7) To establish and maintain close links with all supporting agencies, e.g. school health service, Educational Welfare Service, social services, juvenile liaison officers, community relations officers, NSPCC. This was to be done in conjunction with the headteacher.

(8) To help with the transfer of children to junior or secondary school and liaise with these schools when appropriate.

(9) To make members of staff aware of the customs and practices of the children's home environment.

(10) To foster the full involvement and co-operation of the parents in their children's education.

(11) To form good relationships with colleagues and parents.

(12) To work under the direction of the headteacher in consultation with the appropriate multiracial adviser.

Post-holders had to be experienced teachers, preferably with previous experience of working with pupils for whom English was not their first language.

It seems that many conceptions about home–school liaison work remain firmly fixed in the era of compensatory education. Worse, they reflect confusion about the nature and purposes of popular education.[4] Many initiatives have been taken in response to central government prompting, following a political or social crisis. Often, no one is sure how a particular scheme originates. This occurred in one LEA where I was asked to evaluate a scheme; one headteacher accepted it more or less as a *fait accompli*, feeling that 'somehow my school was picked out'; a second headteacher spoke of 'a phone call out of the blue'. Both of these heads believed the district inspector to have been the main instigator of the scheme. He himself, whilst accepting the role, felt the primary inspectors' team 'responded to the interest in home–school links' that existed in the three schools, especially after he had organised a weekend course on the subject. He felt that the three schools were 'more open' and that the good communications with parents that already existed there should be built upon. In short, he believed he had simply 'made official' what teachers had already been doing voluntarily and unofficially.

Since no one was certain how the scheme had originated the head-teachers naturally had different expectations of it. One felt that 'We had done all we could in school. If more was to be done it had to be before the child entered school. My priority was pre-school.' Another confessed to having 'no real idea' of what to expect but believed himself 'flexible enough' to accept whatever resulted. He felt that the person appointed should be a 'trouble-shooter not a community worker'. Nevertheless, he believed that the appointee had to be a teacher, and this view was strongly and unanimously endorsed. Only a teacher concerned 'with the education of children and with a knowledge of them' would be acceptable to other staff and parents.

This belief, that the liaison worker must be a teacher, continues to be widely held, and the holding of it severely circumscribes the work that can be accomplished. It seems highly desirable that those having the responsibility for recruiting liaison workers should be free to select from candidates with other professional experience than teaching.

Conclusion

The emphasis given in this chapter to the difficulties of defining a role for home–school liaison teachers should be placed against the accounts of excellent work scattered throughout the book. The case history given in Figure 5.2, recorded by an HSLT in a northern city, demonstrates once more that contacts with homes can sometimes improve relationships dramatically – despite the confusion of purposes that often exists. These energetic and dedicated workers deserve better briefing, so that they can exercise their skills to maximum effect.

Figure 5.2

A large family this, with a long history of father domination and ill-kept children. The older children have all needed special education, and father does some community work in playgrounds. He is now living with another woman. They have a son, L., now three years old. I first came in contact with them on a pre-school visit. They have also regularly attended any 'pre-school afternoons' we hold in school.

Mr H. is convinced L. is very intelligent and was distressed to hear we would not give him an IQ test. He wants him to read, too – feels sure he is well above average. As this has been a family we want to keep in close touch with, I helped them out with suggestions for pre-reading work: nursery rhymes, pictures with story under them, tracing, reading him stories, etc. I gave them materials and visited every every few weeks to check how he is progressing. L. is a difficult child, demanding attention (he is the youngest of many). He rarely plays alone, mostly with adults.

However, each time he comes into school he gets better at choosing an activity and playing by himself or with other children. This can be a difficulty for a young child living on the top floor of a block of flats.

The parents now understand the job the nursery does – socially integrating, learning colours, new experiences, singing, etc. – and are assured that if he progresses with his reading when in the infants we will not hold him back waiting for other children; he will work on at his own pace. I feel we have helped to sort out problems which perhaps might have given the nursery and reception teachers a headache.

CHAPTER 6

Lessons to be learned from the communications model

The last quarter of a century has seen numerous, mostly small-scale efforts to redress the balance of disadvantage within the education system. However, judging by the Department of Education's own reports, these efforts have not been very effective. In *Better Schools* (1985), HMI reported:

> In about three-quarters of schools the curriculum is not well planned or effectively put into practice . . . by the end of the primary phase, many pupils have achieved only a shaky foundation for some of their subsequent work, partly because teachers do not always insist that pupils should adequately understand the essentials and partly because they underestimate the pupils' potential . . . in most secondary schools agreed curricular policies appear to have little influence on the whole school.[1]

Whether such one-sided and generalised statements do anything to improve the standards of the schools must be seriously doubted. Well-informed, constructive and practical proposals are required.

The many warnings and calls for action delivered by the worthy committees have not brought about the desired effects. More accurately, they have produced effects, but these have been different from what was intended. The 'system' has certainly moved forward, and some pupils have benefited, but the extravagant hopes that were pinned like flags on the lapels of schools have not, and could not have, been realised. The warning was given that 'schools cannot compensate for society', but it never occurred to most members of the teaching profession that they could. There may be little that schools can do about social conditions like those observed by Willis in Wolverhampton where 'a new class of isolated, depressed and alienated young people has been created by mass unemployment'.[2] A great deal can be done, however, to reduce the effects of educational disadvantage generated in and around schools, to raise the consciousness of parents about the possibilities inherent within the system for its reform or adaptation.

Complexity of the issues

That the efforts to put such measures into effect have not met with greater success can be attributed partly to the complexity of the issues. As has been shown, there is little agreement among the various groups of professionals who have become involved in trying to meet the needs of those in the population designated as disadvantaged. At Downton Park Special School (Chapter 4) there was a sharp and fundamental difference of opinion between the headteacher and a social scientist about the causes and, therefore, about possible solutions. In the absence of conceptual clarity, field projects of this kind drift into a more or less informed pragmaticism not easily distinguishable from what operates when business organisations undergo change, as described by Mangham in 1979:

> in circumstances in which men share power and differ about what must be done, and where these differences are of some consequence, decisions and actions will be the result of a *political* process. It follows that sometimes one group wins, sometimes another; sometimes one individual is able to impose his/her definitions and solutions, sometimes she/he is defeated by another more powerful, more forceful, more persuasive challenger.[3]

The first persuasive voice to make itself heard in the Downton Park project was that of a sociologist, who was engaged as research consultant and produced a report that attributed educational disadvantage almost entirely to the effects of social conditions:

> Children so labelled are seen as having an individual educational problem, when, in fact, they are bearing the burden of all the ills of a technological era, which grow out of history, urbanisation, economic greed, inadequate housing and education, poverty, unemployment, disease and social isolation.[4]

The headteacher responded:

> As an exposé of ESN determinants this report is in parts doctrinaire
> and illogical.

Such divergences are even more apparent in the Swann Report
(1985), which was commissioned to enquire into the education of
children from ethnic-minority groups:

> The central question of how the educational system should respond to
> ethnic diversity evokes, understandably, reactions in which emo-
> tional and political judgements are at least as influential as the sober
> evaluation of evidence . . . The education of the nation's children is a
> matter of profound importance, and the hopes and expectations of
> parents, children and minority communities are, or should be, crucial
> considerations in their own right. The complexity of the issues and
> the range of perceptions associated with them were clearly reflected in
> the Committee's deliberations.[5]

The Swann Committee was set up in 1979 and was riven by dis-
sension from its earliest days. Only eleven of its twenty-nine members served through the whole term; there were nine resignations.
The committee had two chairmen, the first of whom (Mr A.
Rampton) was replaced in May 1981 before the publication, in June,
of its interim report, *West Indian Children in our Schools* (a brief guide
to which is incorporated into the main report as Annexe A). This
first offering from the committee reviewed the findings about West
Indian pupils' school achievement and concluded that *as a group* they
were under-achieving in relation to their peers, not least in obtaining
the examination qualifications to give them equality of opportunity
in the employment market and to enable them to take advantage of
the range of post-school opportunities available. The interim report
considered in some detail the various factors, both inside and outside
the education system, that have been said to cause West Indian children to under-achieve and concluded that racism was the major con-
tributory factor:

> The Committee believes that only a very small minority of teachers
> could be said to be racist in the commonly accepted sense. However,
> it claims that a teacher's attitude towards, and expectations of, West
> Indian pupils may be subconsciously influenced by stereotyped, nega-
> tive or patronising views of their abilities and potential, which may
> prove a self-fulfilling prophecy, and can be seen as a form of "uninten-
> tional racism".[6]

Even the anodyne *Brief Guide* to the *Final* Report, written by Lord Swann in 1985 and distributed to schools – though it avoided mention of racism – referred openly to the enormous frustration and disenchantment with British society among many in the ethnic minority groups: 'Society was not, and still is not, according equality to ethnic minorities. And the education system was not, and still is not, exempt from such criticism.'

The very title of the Swann Report, *Education for All*, affirms that the need is for good quality, anti-racist teaching in all British schools. The report called above all else, for changes in attitudes and behaviour and saw schools as uniquely placed to take a leading role in this process: 'We cannot emphasise too strongly the urgency of the need for change where attitudes to ethnic minorities are concerned.'

Whether the approach currently subsumed under the term 'multicultural education' will have the desired effects must be carefully considered. One influential text[7] – has suggested that the concept revives old attitudes associated with cultural deprivation and compensatory education. This is emphatically not the view of the Swann Report, but one has to note the lukewarm reception and poor quality of the discussion that followed its publication. Few people, whatever their political or ideological commitment, commended it as the significant document it was surely intended to be. That it has been followed by the worst inner-city riots since 1981 has not caused government ministers to refer again to its pages. Yet it is, for the most part, a moderate and sensible report, reflecting the best educational practice in its field. Unless we have reached the position when it has to be said that schools have no substantial part to play in shaping the attitudes and aspirations of the next generation, we have to formulate policies for a multicultural society, and this will involve a fundamental review of concepts like 'multicultural' and, indeed, 'education' itself:

> the aims of education wait to be rewritten . . . the very lack of a definition of multicultural education has permitted not only the widest theoretical interpretations and broadest policy objectives, but also a considerable mismatch between those and educational practices.[8]

The activities of the head and staff of Hamm Green Primary School (Chapter 3) take on a different perspective when seen against a backcloth of political, social and ideological events. Workers in the field are forced to make hourly and daily policy decisions, though they cannot be in possession of much essential data, have no training or special expertise and generally no aspirations towards mould-breaking. If they get it badly wrong, they make convenient scapegoats. The pattern is familiar across all the caring professions. Given these conditions, it seem that the teachers at Hamm Green were performing at a high standard, within a traditional approach that has repeatedly been commended by parents and employers. The approach may have been paternalistic; but although in some ways operating within a compensatory education model, it fulfilled a major requirement of a more advanced model in that it actively cultivated each pupil's educational aspirations and promoted positive attitudes towards the self. Equally, there were unobserved limitations in the school's educational philosophy.

If every primary school in the land were performing like this, we should have a good system; but it would still be necessary to demand answers to some tough questions, which are rarely being asked. Specifically, in the context of this book, the following proposition requires reasoned and sustained discussion: *worthy though the activities are when parents help teachers to achieve goals specified by teachers in ways specified by teachers, a deeper level of parental involvement is required to generate the energy necessary for the regeneration of the British education system in the late twentieth century.*

Enthusiastic and often effective attempts to orientate schools towards their communities have been in progress over the last quarter of a century; but these have been too piecemeal and too dependent on individual initiatives for them to make much impact upon the maintained system generally. Fortunately in a few instances the next step forward has been taken, and the good results achieved support the beliefs that, first, huge untapped reserves of potential exist among learners and, secondly, that techniques exist to enable educators to reach these reserves. The missing crucial ingredient in the formula for effecting the desired social interaction is not denigration of the teaching profession, nor to heap blame on parents, social workers, clergy or anyone else, but to promote trust and self-confidence. To break out of the grip of the mini-measures that have now been tried often enough requires that teachers take small but definite risks. This they cannot do without support and guidance from their local authorities and (since all the major British political parties constantly advocate a greater measure of parental participation in the education system) perhaps from central government too.

The LEA must provide space, time and resources but most of all it must take the risks of allowing local initiative and creativity to blossom. That can mean on occasions that things happen which bend if not break the regulations. It is useful to have a Nelson's eye at such times. But support also means counselling and guiding and protecting, and nurturing further developments.[9]

The above re-statement of commitment from the Director of Education for Coventry was given at a conference in that city, whose long association with policies of community involvement is discussed in the next chapter. Here, and in other examples given in Part Two, it can be seen that many schools have accomplished the shift from a communications to a participatory model. They have succeeded in breaking through the barriers that separated them from their communities and have involved parents in mutually satisfying relationships, some of which have been shown to produce measurable improvements in educational attainment. These successful community educators tend to be very pragmatic people, yet their practice is based upon philosophical and educational ideals that seem far removed from a realistic appraisal of society as it is depicted in the newspapers and in the televised news. On the basis of these observations, one might even ask: what is the justification for continuing to work for greater understanding? I now consider and reject the point-of-view which argues the futility of such efforts.

Is co-operation possible?

A deeply entrenched view (once expounded by the philosopher Hobbes as an argument for absolute sovereignty) is that of man (in the sense of the species) as the human beast, contained only by force or by the threat of force. A 1985 'philosopher' has used the same argument in a letter to the local press:

Discord just human nature

Regarding the Handsworth riots, everyone is asking what can be done to prevent further trouble, and the answer is – nothing. There will always be unrest and problems throughout the country, and it has nothing to do with racism. It is simply human nature.

Trying to get whites, blacks, Asians and Indians [*sic*] to live in harmony is like putting lions and tigers in the same cage. Even when they are born and reared in captivity, and together as cubs, as soon as they are adult they must be separated.

We are merely, the 'superior' species of animal, and the same rules apply. All the talking in the world will not alter this fact.

Realist,
Willenhall[10]

Konrad Lorenz, in his study of aggression – 'the fighting instinct in beast and man which is directed *against* members of the same species' – argues about human behaviour on the basis of his matchless knowledge of the 'territorial fights of the coral fish, the "quasi-moral" urges and inhibitions of social animals, the loveless married and social life of the night heron, the bloody mass–battles of the brown rat'.[11] Lorenz makes a quantum leap (in chapter XII, entitled 'On the Virtue of Scientific Humility') where he asserts as fact human evolution from, and relationships to, the animals. He uses his exposition of a 'parliament of instincts' to explain 'unreasoning and unreasonable human nature' – since, as he observes with the same accuracy as our 'realist' letter-writer, very few transactions between human beings are predominantly determined by reason; 'the ever-recurrent phenomena of history do not have reasonable causes'. All this falls into place like the parts of a jigsaw, 'if one assumes that human behaviour, and particularly human social behaviour, far from being determined by reason and cultural tradition, is still subject to all the laws prevailing in all phylogenetically adapted instinctive behaviour'.

Lorenz does not, however fall into a paroxysm of gloom. On the contrary, he finishes his book with 'an avowal of optimism' and fastens his hopes on a number of strategies for redirecting aggression at substitute objects. High among these strategies are laughter (which 'probably evolved by ritualisation of a redirected threatening movement'), sport and education. Although I cannot follow the leap of reasoning from coral fish to something called 'young people today', and although I never cease to be amazed at the capacity of great 'scientists' (like Freud) to delude themselves that they draw upon empirical evidence when they are simply being great writers and hypothesisers, I am happy that Lorenz reached his cheerful conclusions from such unpromising premises. The Willenhall realist gets his come-uppance in the creed with which this jovial work concludes: 'I believe in the power of human reason as I believe in the power of natural selection. I believe that reason can and will exert a selection pressure in the right direction.'[12]

In a rather better book, Lorenz's pupil Eibl-Eibesfeldt has collected a vast number of examples of positive, social and even altruistic behaviour among birds, fish and the higher vertebrates. He dismisses the theory of the human being's killer nature: 'investigation shows, on the contrary, that by nature we are also extremely friendly beings'.[13]

The ethologists have followed the philosophers. Bertrand Russell wrote courageously in 1917 in the middle of the most destructive war to be seen on earth up till that time, that

> Every man has it in his being to develop into something good or bad; there is a best possible for him, and a worst possible. His circumstances will determine whether his capacities for good are developed or crushed, and whether his bad impulses are strengthened or gradually diverted into better channels.[14]

These circumstances include access to an education system. I conclude that, despite steadily worsening social conditions in Britain, there are still grounds for optimism; that despite the rapid erosion of the state education system, it remains the only viable delivery service for a counter-attack against prejudice and hatred. Nevertheless, many notions still regarded as non-problematic need to be re-examined.

Even the aims and purposes of universal education remain unclear. Universal education is, historically speaking, a recent innovation and has not been realised fully anywhere in the world, though some Scandinavian countries may have come near to achieving that ideal. There is some disagreement about whether education can in fact be made available to everyone. Some have argued that education is an initiation into worthwhile activities and that entry into the citadel of learning may, by definition, be limited to those who possess or can acquire the capacities necessary to succeed in predetermined initiation rites. There seems no good reason, however, why education should be associated with exclusion:

> Our concept of an educated person is of someone who is capable of delighting in a variety of pursuits and projects for their own sake and whose pursuit of them and general conduct of his/her life are transformed by some degree of all-round understanding and sensitivity . . .
> . . . being educated is a desirable state to be in, for those for whom it functions as an ideal, because of the ways in which value can be ascribed to the pursuit and possession of knowledge – i.e. as an absorbing and challenging activity, as illuminating other pursuits, and as incorporating the intrinsic value of truth.[15]

Few practitioners, parents or pupils would identify their experience of school with such a view of the process of education. Yet it would not be wise to dismiss such ideals as lacking relevance, either for the education system in general or for those entering it under disadvantaged conditions. The ideal of 'education for all' has re-appeared as the title of the Swann Report (1985); the Warnock Report on the education of children with special needs (1978) re-affirmed that 'the purpose of education for all children is the same, the goals are the same. But the help that individual children need in progressing towards them will be different.'[16] A lofty, high-profile view of the education process has also been taken by those seeking to combat the very much worse problems faced, for example, in China and Latin America, and by those who mounted the Experimental World Literacy Programme, which derives its ideas from the work of Paulo Freire.[17] But there is little common ground between the different pedagogical theories that have been built upon these ideals. Some theories are concerned with maintaining 'standards' through the exclusion of 'incompetents', transferring resources to citadels of learning, which shut out those who cannot pass entry rituals. Others emphasise the drawing out of undiscovered talents, dialogue and problem-solving methods, and open access: 'trust in the people, faith in men and in the creation of a world in which it will be easier to love' – Freire's words would be echoed by most community educators.[18]

Community education past and future

Community education, broadly conceived and boldly executed, offers hope and new perspectives on old problems. It is blind to age, gender and ethnic group, deaf to the murmurs, or shouts, of those who like to label people or lump them together in dubious categories around such dead concepts as 'intelligence'. Community education aims to promote the personal and social development of all people living in a defined geographical area. It reflects a view of education (1) that is lifelong, (2) in which the participants should be actively and influentially involved and (3) in which the needs of the participants determine the nature and timing of provision. A concept so broad and wide-reaching can be applied to all stages of education, including full-time education in schools and colleges. Were each of these elements to be given due weight and serious consideration, the concept might start to turn the education world upside-down. Our world is being turned upside-down anyway, with massive changes in the distribution of available work and new attitudes to leisure.

A voice from the past

It is usual to commence an account of the history of community education with Henry Morris, and it is true that his work in Cambridge-shire has turned out to have had a strange and possibly enduring influence.[19] It might well have appeared to a sophisticated observer of the educational scene of the 1930s and 1940s that Morris had set out to remedy a defective educational system in one particular and largely uninfluential sector of society, and that the experiment, though extremely interesting, was of limited significance in other areas of the country. However, such an observer would have been wrong because the notions hatched in Cambridgeshire were carried into Leicestershire by Stuart Mason (who worked briefly with Morris before the Second World War) and Andrew Fairbairn.

The first village college was at Sawston in Cambridgeshire in 1930; the first in Leicestershire was established in 1964. By the 1970s Morris's ideas had been thoroughly implemented in Leicestershire and have been so well documented that the LEA has published a bibliography of writings about its education system. Community colleges have been set up in many parts of England and Wales: Madeley Court in Telford, Abraham Moss in Manchester, Stantonbury in Buckinghamshire, the Sutton Centre in Nottinghamshire. An especially well documented school has been Countesthorpe in Leicestershire, and no one reading John Watts could fail to be moved by the dedication, verve, imagination, flexibility and general get-up-and-go that are revealed as characteristic of this school.[20] Also well documented has been the Sutton Centre, which was the subject of a long-term evaluation; the researchers concluded: 'Education at Sutton Centre, far from being a hotch-potch of novel ideas and fads, is in fact a co-ordinated and consistent programme working to clear educational goals.'[21]

So there can be no question but that the seeds sown fifty years ago in Cambridgeshire have produced strong growth, and that there is a continued interest in the concept of community education. This has spread to urban schools. Among the most thoroughgoing experiments in community education have been those conducted in Coventry. Their theoretical foundations are an amalgam of the ideas generated in the 1960s and 1970s by projects such as EPA; the Community Development project and various Schools Council Projects; but the main thrust has been practical rather than theoretical; it has looked at ways of linking home and school in both directions and has produced numerous useful publications intended for parents and pupils. Coventry has designated a number of its secondary schools as community schools and through a powerful and determined administrative team has succeeded in establishing a strong tradition of community involvement in the educational process.

A hope for the future

The concept of education has broadened. The notion of lifelong education, both formal and informal, has been fully accepted, even by those who are reluctant to spend money on it. Education is increasingly seen as a continuing process, and community education is concerned with people of all ages from pre-school to old age. Nobody disputes that people made redundant early in their working lives require retraining and the opportunity to qualify themselves for new occupations. Indeed, a strong statement on the need for 'flexibility' forms part of every educational philosopher's programme for the 1980s. In those parts of the country where the consequences of unemployment are most starkly evident, the main hope often resides in people's capacity to generate their own work. The implications of structural changes in society – which are not confined to Britain or even the EEC, but are in some respects world-wide – have not begun to be absorbed. When they have been, the opportunities presented must be seized at the same time as the problems generated are being tackled. Community education is directly concerned with both the opportunities and the problems.

Bernard Harvey, a Leicestershire adviser, has suggested two roles for community education in a changing society:

(1) equipping people to cope, to understand and to find security in society;
(2) enabling people to take part in and influence all the processes of change.

Community education in this tradition is school-based but looks outwards, so that teachers who work in such schools require new and different skills, few of which are inculcated during teacher training. How are newly qualified graduates supposed to have become competent to visit parents in their homes, to take just one practical example from a well-known community college that has introduced such a scheme? Nicholas Gillett, then of the University of Bristol, suggested in 1979 that teachers, and those in related professions, can best be prepared for community education by in-service training:

> They need to learn how to make a thorough study of the educational resources of an area – from retired experts and volunteers from among mothers to sources of scrap materials. They also need to undertake a systems analysis of the situation in which they are working . . . each of these studies can be aided by a knowledge of psychology and sociology . . . they need some acquaintance with community development which embodies ideas about change and the future, and experience of social survey and of work camps or community service.[22]

Because few, if any, of the skills required by teachers engaging in such a programme could have been acquired during initial training, an important aspect of this approach is to make teacher-training establishments themselves more aware of community education.

There is general agreement that community education courses must, above all, be *practical*. However, as Eric Midwinter has remarked:

> Community education has a dual connotation . . . . It is, on the one hand, recognised as a vital concept to which many people pay lip-service and which is acknowledged as having a meaningful role to play in our educational system over the next generations. And yet, on the other hand, it is a terribly vague concept which, although recognised by all, is not easy to grasp. The two words – community and education – must be among the most difficult in the language to define.[23]

Some broad approaches to such courses are given in Figure 6.1.

There seems no necessity to delve further into the term 'community', since it has been defined operationally in the preceding chapters. But the challenge of the term 'education' is taken up in Parts Two and Three. It has become increasingly evident that those local authorities that consider community involvement schemes too expensive soon find themselves paying a great deal more in other ways. Britain has experienced riots and serious breakdowns between cultural groups, and the attempt to reconstitute a sense of

Figure 6.1 Guidelines for constructing community education courses
Attitudes (awareness, perspectives)
Is the course likely to develop the following attitudes?

(1) Sensitivity to the existence of varied cultures in a multi-ethnic community.
(2) Commitment to the education of people of all ages, abilities, needs, social and ethnic groupings in both formal and informal learning contexts.
(3) Commitment to the continuous assessment of their own professional performance.

Skills

(4) Does the course contain adequate external, practical skill-training elements in community education?
(5) Is this practical work relevant? Does it facilitate the development of the skills defined as being essential for success in community education?
(6) What provision is there for ensuring that 'practice' is influenced in a dynamic manner by the theoretical components of the course?
(7) Can you give some practical examples of the skills required under headings such as:

- organisational;
- interactionist – ability to interact with people of different social and cultural background, ages and ability?
- evaluative techniques?
- learning and teaching techniques?

Knowledge

(8) Does the course have a theoretical context that will provide a firm foundation for the development of the above attitudes and skills?
(9) Does the theoretical content of the course facilitate successful learning during the practical component?
(10) Does it include specific knowledge of:

- the range of philosophies within community education;
- the range of practice within community education and its historical development;
- the culture of different groups, especially those resident in Britain;
- the personal development of children, adolescents and adults;
- the learning processes of people of different ages and ability?

community is no longer confined to idealists. There must be better ways to achieve it than by fighting local and civil wars; there are surely educational means of contributing towards the process.

PART TWO

Towards Participation

Our hope of salvation lies in our being surprised by the other. Let us learn always to receive further surprises.
                    Ivan Illich, *Celebration of Awareness*

Children, when a book is boring, yawn openly. They don't expect their writers to redeem humanity, but leave to adults such childish illusions.
Isaac Bashevis Singer, speech on receiving the Nobel Prize for Literature, 1978

CHAPTER 7

Collaborative learning: a whole-system approach

The Coventry Community Education Project (1969–85)

Coventry, unlike some local education authorities that take part in community development projects, has sustained this innovation. It has given community education a permanent place within its Education Service, since it originated in 1971 as part of the national (Home Office) Community Development Project, which was established to revive communities in disadvantaged areas. The Community Education Project (CEP) consisted in its infancy of a small team placed in an infant school in the heart of the city's multi-ethnic and disadvantaged area. Its work ranged over twelve primary schools and a nursery centre and involved the Sidney Stringer Community School. The team provided additional support and innovative services to teachers, pupils and parents in the area by:

- developing a programme in schools designed to encourage home–school and community–school links;
- developing in-service training and support programmes for teachers in the use of the latest teaching techniques, the development of communication skills, and understanding the culture of people in the inner-city area;
- supporting teachers in their first year from college;
- developing an adult programme seeking to respond to community needs rather than present the community with additional education possibilities offered from an institution;

- establishing a home tutoring scheme for mothers;
- assisting with the extension of pre-school provision.

   In 1975 the idea of a 'decentralised' team was replicated in four other areas of the city. These areas were selected on the basis of degree of disadvantage suffered by the pupils in the schools, thus retaining the original 'positive discrimination' policy. Community education strategies were developed in each area. These differed in detail, but all regarded home–school relationships as a priority. The following account is drawn from documents published by the education authority.[1]

Home–school

Strategies and support materials have been developed that have widened, deepened and informalised parental involvement in many of the schools concerned. Parents are being accepted as genuine partners in the educational process. The following list gives some idea of the kind of activity that occurs right across the city: parents' rooms, family clubs, dressmaking, English lessons, school youth clubs, subject evenings e.g. modern maths, tea afternoons, do-it-yourself evenings, film nights, discos, social evenings, lunchtime concerts, craft club evenings, keep-fit classes.

Pre-school

Mother-and-toddler groups have been developed in many schools, as well as ready-for-school groups and a wide range of home-visiting strategies. The training element in these strategies has laid the foundation for adult education work. In 1973, the Van Leer Foundation provided a grant for an experimental scheme using local mothers, trained and supervised by qualified teachers, to run annexes to the Hillfields Nursery Centre. Three years later the Foundation offered to provide sufficient additional funds to enable the scheme to be extended to a second area for a three-year period.

Adult education

From informal beginnings, dealing with a content mainly concerned with the development and education of young children, a more formal provision has developed. Courses on local history, simple graphics, Indian dancing and GCE O-level English are examples of provision made at several primary schools. Many adults attend regular classes in day schools to study for O- and A-level examinations. Leadership courses are also being run to train some parents to take over the leadership of a wide variety of groups in schools. This generation of self-help skills is further exemplified by the training of a multiracial group of parents who carry out home-visiting duties in their school catchment area. These visitors work under the direction of the school headteacher and in close liaison with health visitors and social workers. Some schools have begun to evolve a parents' syllabus from their home–school programmes. Each school's syllabus is structured to ensure that during their time with the school, parents will be given a share in most aspects of the curriculum side by side with their child's progress through the school.

Curriculum

Materials have been devised to encourage situations in which parents, children and teachers work together on the development of observation, analysis, diagnosis and social action skills in terms of the local environment. Four of the five city areas have seen the influence of the community on the curriculum as a priority, which is exhibited in several patterns: using the local community as a starting-point for wider urban studies or taking a particular aspect of the community as the basis for developing a specific curriculum strategy. Various teaching kits have evolved out of these initiatives. Particular interest has been centred on the teaching of reading skills and has resulted in the production of a highly-structured and monitored scheme to measure and describe the effects of parental involvement in a school-directed reading programme, of pre-school reading materials, of booklets specifically designed to stimulate parental involvement in a school reading programme, and of reading books containing children's imaginative stories.

Home-tutoring services for Asian adults have been operating throughout the period under review, and families in many parts of the city are in receipt of regular help. In addition there have been a variety of afternoon and evening classes, regularly attended by more than one hundred women, with many more attending occasionally as and when other commitments have permitted. Other activities of the Community Education Project have included the provision of in-service training for teachers, the publication of regular communication links with schools – bulletins, news-sheets, staff-room folders, etc. – and holiday playtime schemes engaging the practical support of students attending Lanchester Polytechnic and Warwick University.

This, then, was the public image of the CEP at the time I began to have access to the schools for an evaluation study (see below).

Many primary schools were attempting to create an atmosphere conducive to the development of reading: book displays were arranged throughout schools; community assemblies were organised based on stories, new library books, etc.; community libraries based in schools were run by parents and other community members; slides, film-strips and films of stories were shown to parents and pupils. Children were allowed to take home any books in the school except those borrowed from the city library. Books taken home were treated as something special and so were transported to and from school in a specially prepared plastic folder. In addition to the child's reading book, many schools also made available a selection of very attractive books for children to choose from. Although these books were generally arranged roughly according to readability level, the children were free to make their own choices.

Pre- and early-reading and language workshops for parents had been run by some schools. There had been many local radio broadcasts, 'listening groups' and phone-ins, followed up by discussion groups in local schools.

Reading, in an extended form that includes many aspects of language development, had always featured prominently in the Coventry CEP programme. In the early 1970s, under the leadership of John Rennie, a city-wide scale of activities was achieved. School work was displayed on buses, and public figures were associated with the programme, which focused on school activities of all kinds, especially reading and mathematics. Children whose work was used then were by now in their twenties, and many had pre-school children themselves. Thus in some parts of the city two generations had experience of schools that had encouraged them to take direct action in relation to their own lives, as well as making a positive contribution towards the psychological and educational development of children.

Community schools and educational standards

Is there any evidence that schools which go out of their way to provide such a welcome to parents achieve a measurable effect on children's attainments? An opportunity arose to evaluate the effects of a current CEP language development initiative. This study was published under the title *Raising Standards*;[2] its main findings do, at last, provide some grounds for optimism. The programmes were at different stages. Some schools had been following open-door policies for a decade; others were more recently involved, which meant that we were looking at both the long-term and short-term effects of programmes initiated by the Coventry CEP teacher advisers. They identified eight schools (plus an infants department) that were particularly welcoming and effective in integrating parental contributions in many different ways. The classic research design we had hoped to achieve was not feasible, and instead we studied schools selected from this sample that were known effectively to involve parents.[3]

The Hunter–Grundin Literacy Profiles used for the study consist of five tests; four group tests assessing attitudes to reading, reading for meaning, spelling and free writing; and one individual test assessing spoken language. None of the tests takes longer than ten minutes to complete. Despite the importance attributed to reading, it is desirable that progress should be assessed on a wide spectrum of language skills. The Hunter–Grundin battery uses a picture as a stimulus to conversation and distinguishes five elements in oral language at infants' level: confidence, enunciation, vocabulary, accuracy and imagination. These are assessed using a five-point scale. Older children can be assessed on their free-writing performance, using measures of legibility, fluency, accuracy and originality. These are also assessed on a five-point scale. Additionally, the profiles provide a measure of attitudes towards reading. Level 1 is intended for use at the end of the children's infant schooling, i.e. around the age of seven years. Level 2 is intended for use after one year in the junior school, i.e. around the age of eight. Level 3 contains scales for the nine- to ten-year-olds. Levels 4 and 5 are also available.

The results of the evaluation study may be summarised as follows.

Spoken language among infants

One hundred and sixteen children were individually tested, using the picture stimulus provided. The conversations that ensued were either tape-recorded and transcribed or taken down directly in shorthand.

Confidence: 81 per cent of the pupils in this sample (which included a large number who have to be categorised as 'socially disadvantaged' according to criteria usually accepted)[4] were able to respond in a one-to-one test situation with a strange adult without signs of anxiety.

Enunciation: more than 90 per cent were categorised as having 'intelligible speech' and more than half as possessing 'precise and carefully enunciated speech'.

Vocabulary: nearly 80 per cent of the children used 35 or more words, and 32 per cent used 65 or more. Vocabulary is one of the most widely used measures in assessments of infant schoolchildren, and the results usually show the 'socially disadvantaged' as performing poorly. Terms like 'verbally destitute' have been applied to this population. In the sample studied the children showed a confident attitude towards adults, and talked freely to a strange visitor who took notes; and when they did so their use of language fell within normal limits.

Free writing

Samples were collected from cohorts of 7-, 8- and 9-year-olds. These were graded according to a system provided in the test manuals, which identifies the following elements: legibility, fluency, accuracy, originality. The proportion of children scoring high on each element increased at each year group; by nine years, over 90 per cent could write legibly, and nearly as many fluently and accurately. The only negative aspect was that on the measures of accuracy and originality the results suggested there were few 'high fliers'.

Attitudes to reading

Unusually for schools designated social priority schools (SPS) a very high proportion of infants (74 per cent) and junior (86 per cent) children revealed positive attitudes towards reading.

Reading for meaning

Level 1 in the Hunter–Grundin profiles corresponds to a chronological age of about eight years, Level 2 to nine years and Level 3 to ten years. Mean differences between Levels 1 and 2 were statistically significant overall ($p<.001$), indicating a massive improvement in reading attainment within the schools and between these separate cohorts. This gain was sustained in the second year, although the rate of increase diminished.

The mean scores for the Coventry sample were compared by socio-economic groupings with those provided in the test manuals. At Level 1 the Coventry means were consistently below those of the Hunter–Grundin. At Levels 2 and 3 they were significantly better ($p<.001$). *The overall Coventry means were, in fact, equal or superior to those of the 'middle-class' schools.* These were unexpected results. The population of the EPA/SPS schools included a high proportion of non-white pupils (in one school 84 per cent were from an Asian ethnic group).

One – perhaps the only – useful purpose served by normative testing is to allow a school system to compare its pupils with scores obtained from a national sample. The tests were adminstered strictly according to protocol. Such achievement at many different age levels and in so many different aspects of language development cannot be dismissed as mere chance.[4]

Summary

For many years now schools in Coventry have given top priority to involving parents throughout their children's school career, particularly in the areas of reading and language development. The study covering eight of these schools and nearly one thousand pupils living in disadvantaged areas revealed high levels of achievement in oral and written language and in reading comprehension. Attitudes to reading were generally positive. Age-related reading scores were better among older children. Comparisons with national norms provided in the test manuals showed that some levels of achievement in the Coventry schools were significantly better than the norms provided for 'middle-class' children. Good-quality written work was found at eight, nine and ten years; the latter age band had more than 90 per cent who could write 'legibly', 'fluently' and 'accurately'.

These results are extremely encouraging, although they do not 'prove' that involving parents in this way has a direct bearing on children's reading and language performance. It is nevertheless legitimate to note the association between long-term parental involvement programmes of this sort and the good results obtained, and that in a follow-up study in three of the same schools there was a significant trend associating higher reading scores with greater support from parents. The results certainly scotch the idea that allowing parents free access to schools diminishes educational attainment. On the contrary, schools that have followed such policies have obtained higher scores than the national norms, and in the basic subjects too.

CHAPTER 8

Parents, language and reading development

So far, certain aspects of the drive to involve parents in their children's reading development have been described. By reviewing a study of parental involvement programmes in Coventry schools (Chapter 7) it has been possible to discuss some of the emerging trends and suggest ways in which schools might move further ahead. It appears that programmes following the grain of the Plowden-inspired primary school,[1] that apply socio-linguistic policies and practices to reading development, will produce good results; such schemes are likely to raise levels of educational achievement among 'disadvantaged' populations. However, more sophisticated programmes should now be developed, bringing together out-of-school learning, individual differences among children and parental contributions into consistent language policies right through the infant and junior schools.

How widespread is the present movement to involve parents in their children's reading? What do schools hope to achieve by involving parents in the learning-to-read process? How do they go about it? What problems do they experience (or anticipate experiencing)? What measures do they take to prevent these difficulties arising or to minimise their effects should they arise? Given that children have been encouraged to take books home for decades (a Schools Council project found in 1976 that, irrespective of social category, 87 per cent of the parents interviewed were in favour of this, and well over half the children in a large, well-chosen sample were already doing so), what is new in the present 'growth industry'? Where do we go from here? The following investigation of these questions derives from (1) observations in the course of evaluating parental involvement programmes in several different parts of England, (2) a national survey (see below) and (3) the study of parental involvement programmes in Coventry schools described in the previous chapter.

How widespread is parent involvement?

A national survey in 1983 began with an enquiry sent to most local educational authorities in Britain, asking if there were schools that were actively involving parents in reading.[2] Fifty-five infant and junior schools were identified and returned detailed questionnaires. These schools covered nearly the whole gamut of social class and had a geographical spread from the Western Isles of Scotland to eastern England, as the following examples show.

Six schools described themselves as being in working–class urban areas; one said that all its pupils lived in rented accommodation and that unemployment was at a very high level. Another said half its children were living with one parent only or with a step-parent. In one school 48 per cent of the pupils were said to be 'immigrants', and 25 per cent of these required teaching in English as a second language; four other schools had no such facilities, although one had pupils from seventeen different nationalities. Four schools had mixed council and private housing; three drew almost exclusively on catchment areas containing privately owned housing. One of the latter said its children almost invariably attended play-groups and that numbers of them would, at the age of 6 or 7, go to independent schools.

These pockets of activity appeared to spring from the initiatives of individual schools and in some cases individual teachers. Sometimes, as in the London boroughs of Croydon and Hackney, in Derbyshire and in Coventry, groups of schools were joining together to share experiences and resources, but the picture generally was of disparate, autonomous initiatives. It nevertheless proved possible to identify some patterns both in approaches to the teaching of reading and in rationales provided for involving parents.

Approaches to the teaching of reading

Despite their many differences in accommodation, social class of
parents and catchment areas, there was a considerable degree of
unanimity in that virtually all the schools placed reading in the context of a language policy. A very eclectic mixture of methods to teach
reading was reported; look-and-say, phonics, the use of context cues
and a language experience approach, and so on.

A similar disparity was apparent in the classroom arrangements.
Most schools seemed to generate an informal atmosphere in the
class, while following a fairly 'structured' approach. Mostly teaching was given in small groups, with occasional teaching on a one-to-
one basis. There was general encouragement for children to talk to
teachers, and this dialogue, written down, was sometimes used as a
source of reading material. Personal reading books were thus con-
structed and printed by the local resources centre to make them look
attractive and special. Reading games were widely used. Whole-class
teaching was not used, except for specific purposes. The overall
impression was of flexibility in method and approach, and a general
acceptance of a language experience philosophy masking considerable differences in emphasis. These ranged from usage of basal readers to virtually a free choice of books. Not one school seemed to be
relying heavily on phonics. All the schools tried to extend reading to
other subject areas. Story books were displayed in class to encourage
reading for pleasure, and visits were made to local libraries. Some
teachers provided word lists or dictionaries of useful words for topic
work, which pupils could supplement. Reading for meaning and
reference and index skills were built into all curriculum areas in one
school. Class projects used the school library, and schools often
liaised with the local library service. Silent reading and reading aloud
were included in all subject areas in most schools.

Goals and methods

The schools hoped that involving parents in their children's reading
would give the pupils more practice and a sense of achievement, that
it would increase their enjoyment in reading and help them become
fluent sooner. This would have benefits across the curriculum as well

as helping them to see that reading was not just a school activity.
Other hoped-for effects on schools and teachers were:

- A better atmosphere in school and hence a better learning environment.
- An active partnership between parents and teachers in order to meet the educational needs of as many pupils as possible.
- A better understanding by teachers of parents' concerns and a realisation that parents might not have the knowledge that schools sometimes take for granted.
- Agreement between parents and teachers meaning that children would have no divided loyalties.
- More time spent in direct teaching if parents are hearing the children read, allowing teachers to foster new approaches to reading.
- Involvement of people other than parents, such as grandparents, aunts, friends and relatives.

All of the schools that provided information were attempting to involve parents in a variety of ways. Parents were generally encouraged to visit the school to see the children's work, and one school set aside a specific time for this activity. Parents became involved in various activities, such as crafts and cookery, and in others that some schools could not otherwise provide, such as pottery and other specialised areas of the curriculum. Parents helped in classrooms with creative work, reading and number games and were invited to attend asemblies. Some schools had regular meetings with groups of parents in the form of mothers' groups, English-as-a-second-language groups, mother-tongue groups and parent–teacher associations. Some schools encouraged parents to help in the school library or office. A minority of schools had a parents' room, and in some instances parents studied at the school doing O- or A-levels or Open University courses.

As far as reading was concerned, the vast majority of these schools opted for a system that established an agreement between the parents and the school that they would hear the child read regularly and would note this fact on the card provided – together with any suitable comments. Parents were in general discouraged from teaching decoding strategies, and instead encouraged to delay attention to errors, use context clues and offer praise for success. This approach is popular because it fits relatively easily into the normal classroom routine. It is thought by teachers to be manageable since it provides a specific task for the parents and children and helps to structure parental involvement.

An important side-effect of involving parents is that it forces a school to reconsider its policy towards reading and to reorganise its materials for systematic use by 'outsiders'. (This usually results in a wider range of reading materials – both fiction and non-fiction being made available to the pupils – which, in turn, is likely to enhance the acquisition of higher-order reading skills.) For many schools this produces a radical departure from previous practice and it is one answer to a question posed at the beginning of this chapter – What is new in the present 'growth industry' of parental involvement in reading? Extra resources, well organised and strategically placed throughout the school, may in themselves go some way towards explaining increments in reading generally associated with parental involvement programmes.

Problems and how they may be tackled

The schools were frank about the difficulties they had experienced or anticipated experiencing. These problems included the following:

- Some parents were not really interested in reading.
- Over-anxious parents could push children too hard.
- Some parents enjoyed challenging and contradicting teachers.
- Some parents themselves were illiterate or barely literate.
- A shortage of books was a problem mentioned several times.
- Some parents were unwilling to co-operate; others were interested for a short while, but their enthusiasm soon waned.
- Domestic crises could affect whether or not parents heard children read at home.
- Some parents could not cope with even the simplest recording method; others over-reacted to its importance.
- At one school parents became so 'emotive' that it was thought 'necessary' to exclude all parents who were not qualified teachers from hearing their children read at home! At another, parents found it difficult to distinguish between involvement and actual teaching.
- Some parents might well make unfavourable comments about a particular child to his or her own parents.

Measures adopted by schools to prevent such problems arising or to minimise their consequences have included the following:

- Pre-admission visits were arranged and parents were encouraged to visit the school – both measures intended to foster interest among parents.
- Parents' clubs were organised to discuss problems.
- Extra books were acquired, and extra meetings were arranged so that problems could be discussed.
- Parents engaged in fund-raising activities in order to purchase more books.
- Parents were given detailed advice as to what they could usefully do when listening to their child read.
- Other tasks could be found for the parents who were not really interested in reading. It is important to identify parents' strengths and to utilise these. 'A parent who is very good in one situation may be uncomfortable in another'; 'One approach will not meet the needs of all parents and children – one must, therefore, be open, flexible and prepared to consider a variety of approaches.'

So what's new?

The reasons given by schools for involving parents fall into two broad categories, although these categories were not necessarily mutually exclusive. Some schools emphasised the contribution of teachers as professionals and believed that by making the teacher's expertise available to parents it would be possible to extend the input of 'good' teaching methods. Such intervention programmes carry the underlying assumption that professionals know how parents should interact with, and educate, their children. This was a matter of great concern to Raven.[3] Tizard and Hughes were similarly worried that teachers' advice could encourage parents to behave like teachers.[4] These researchers were not against parental involvement, however, provided it was at an appropriate level and sensitively implemented:

> Almost all parents respond with interest when someone knowledgeable shows an individual concern for their child and points out to them aspects of her development which they had been unaware of. We can therefore see a useful role for parents' groups, and for advice and

information centres which respond to these needs, but none for attempts by professionals to alter the way in which parents carry out their education role.[5]

Most of the schools observed or that provided information saw parental involvement as a two-way process. Teachers openly admitted that they, not just the parents and the pupils, had benefited as a consequence, both professionally and personally. This was the other main reason given for parental involvement.

A considerable disparity of methods and emphasis was apparent; but the vast majority of teachers were following an approach to the teaching of reading that could broadly be described in the terms used by Ferreiro and Teberosky: 'reading is not deciphering, and writing is not copying' (or more precisely, reading is more than just deciphering and writing is more than just copying).[6] Most teachers were basing the learning-to-read process on the belief that children do not make progress mechanically. Rather, they make progress as they acquire concepts of what the reading process is – which leads in turn to an awareness that meanings are incorporated in the written word. Strong efforts were made to relate reading and writing to the children's oral language and everyday experience. 'Breakthrough to Literacy', a scheme that lends itself naturally to this approach, was widely used in conjunction with a broad range of back-up materials.[7] This strong emphasis on matching the symbols on the page to the child's oral language made it easier for the child, who was, in effect, being asked to make sense of his or her own experiences. The effect appeared similar even when the system in use was described as 'paired reading', which is usually regarded as originating in the behaviourist school of psychology.

It is probable that the good results achieved through these approaches have nothing to do with technique or behaviourism. They are, in fact, adequately explained by the psychoanalysts Bettelheim and Zelan during an account of their own, non-interventionist procedures for helping emotionally disturbed children overcome reading difficulties. They suggest that a positive attitude promotes reading because it is based on a 'reciprocal agreement that enhances the child's self-respect around reading'.[8] Work observed in Salford and Leicester emphasised this positive attitude, which included training parents, during two visits to homes, using the following printed instructions:[9]

Stage One   Paired reading
(1) Choose a book.
(2) Read the words together, simultaneously.
(3) If the child hesitates over a word say what it is. The child repeats the word and then you carry on reading together. Don't say 'No' or 'You've got it wrong' – just carry on reading.
(4) Read together for 5 minutes only 5 times a week for 2 weeks.
(5) If the child wishes, re-read the book – otherwise choose a new one.
(6) At the end of the reading session praise the child and talk about what you have read.
[Given on first visit.]

Stage Two   Independent reading
(1) Choose a book.
(2) Read it together as before. When the child feels able to read without the parent, the child knocks. This tells the parent to stop reading.
(3) When the child makes a mistake or is unable to read, the parent gives the correct word. The child repeats it. Continue to read together until the next knock.
(4) Praise the child for knocking and independent reading. Pay no attention to the child's mistake.
[Given on second visit]

Such an approach to parental involvement in reading contains a blend of formal and informal mould-breaking methods. Flexibility and positive attitudes were enhanced by the use of many reading games and activities demonstrated to parents at special gatherings, or in some instances by bringing the parent into the classroom during school-time. Children who were asked about this experience soon ceased to mention the 'knocking' technique, talking instead about the games and the books they were reading:

LEE: I like *Funny Bones* as well. That was about skelingtons that came out at night and a dog that broke his bones so they had to fix him up together, but they did not know how to fix him up together.
NITESH: The story of *Burglar Bill* was a man named Burglar Bill used to go out every night and steal every important person's things – whatever he gets hold of.
LEE: *Flat Stanley* is about a boy that was very flat. He could go under a door and go through drains. One day his . . . his . . . mum lost her ring down the drain so he asked his mum get a piece of string

and tied it to his hand. So Flat Stanley he went down the drain and he
. . . an he got the ring. I liked the games. Every week we took, every
week we took a game home, It's a lot of fun (pause) er (pause) my
favourite game is the Dragon game (pause), but I got Scrabble now. I
like Scrabble a lot.

NITESH: I like the Dragon game. It is good and we have to play it
going down the dragon and we pick a card up and read the thing
and it says numbers and all that.

LEE: Then me and Nitesh made a game of Scrabble of our own.

NITESH: It was quite fun. I like making games. I made a sort of pocket
to put our little bits of (pause) *C* and all little bits of letters in.[10]

As we read these transcripts of the children's accounts of the paired
reading scheme in Leicester, it becomes evident that the interactions
described have moved into the realm of participation. All notions of
'compensation' have been left behind; in fact, a new style of co-
operative learning is being forged. In addition to the community
aspect, which is significant, there may well be methodological implications that have not yet begun to be explored in any systematic way,
especially the attitude to the children's errors that is being inculcated.
Whatever nuances of the 'paired reading' programme are
emphasised (and there are many, as has been shown), they all train
the parent (or surrogate) not to comment on the child's errors but
immediately to offer a further correct model. In accepting children's
misreadings, enthusiasts for this approach may well have stumbled
on an important learning principle.

Gordon Wells believes that middle-class children do well in the
early years of schooling because they come to school already used to
books and to seeing the written word at work.[11] By making written
language more relevant to the disadvantaged child's pre-school
experience, schools are attempting to adapt their teaching methods
to overcome this lack of response to the written word. This approach
can be complemented by making books more accessible to homes
through lending libraries in local schools, a 'book-bus', a home-
based early learning project and a variety of other strategies. Most
teachers would accept research findings indicating that parental
intervention is important to a child's linguistic competence – which
is, in turn, crucial to later development.[12] One of the more disturb-
ing observations made by Tizard and Hughes was that children who
were learning and thinking successfully at home were unable to
transfer their skills to the school environment.[12] It seems, therefore,

that schools have a great responsibility to seek better co-operation with homes so that they can get to know families more intimately and appreciate and build on the progress children have made at home. Such procedures are well developed in Coventry, where members of the CEP have devised a family curriculum incorporating child- and family-centred methods of teaching, a structured programme giving parents a continuous opportunity to share in the teaching of all or most aspects of the curriculum during their seven-year association with a primary school. The regular presence of adults in the Coventry schools may help to explain the children's confidence while experiencing a formal spoken language test. Children were encouraged to talk and discuss issues with adults other than their own class teacher. This provided opportunities for them to formulate and pose pertinent questions and to find alternative ways of expressing themselves clearly and accurately. Stories and poems, which Wells believes enhance the development of abstract thought, were being told or read by community members; this was particularly common where stories were required to be told in a language other than English.

There is little doubt that performance in many areas of language development can be considerably improved through parental involvement. The studies cited have shown that parents of disadvantaged children can be readily involved despite their many personal difficulties. Obstacles to reading that are broadly categorised as 'motivational' can be resolved through these programmes. However, problems do arise in sustaining the impetus of the 'head-start' language programmes and continuing them systematically through the junior school. Even so, most of the schools observed were making strenuous efforts towards developing parental involvement in conjunction with language development policies. Much has been achieved, and the way forward seems clear: foster a deeper awareness and understanding of out-of-school learning so that the professionals as well as the parents can develop and build on what children already know; take more account of individual differences, in particular children with specific learning difficulties; look more closely at parental contributions to language policies so that higher-order study skills can be acquired. Then it might be possible to sustain the spurts in achievement that are regularly recorded early in many children's school lives but are not reflected in performance at secondary level.

The Coventry schools were taking part in a scheme whose starting-point was the Plowden Report (1967). They were putting into practice two of that report's main proposals: the notion of positive discrimination and the notion of the community school. Language policies were also developed in response to the recommendations of the Bullock Report (1975). Primary schools that wish to review their collective attitudes towards reading and language development might find the following guidelines helpful as a basis for organising staff meetings. The checklist forms a useful structure for a survey of current school policies (or their absence). A pro forma for recording successful *practice* is suggested in Chapter 9, Figure 9.2.

Check-list for discussion of a school's language policy

(1) READING AND LANGUAGE DEVELOPMENT

Principles and practices

What strategies are being developed to establish principles and policies for reading and language development?

- Are staff familiar with the most important policy statements, such as the Bullock Report and the Swann Report, and any local authority guidelines?
- Do existing frameworks, such as a special responsibility post for language development, appear to be working well?
- Has 'policy' been achieved through specially created groups, like working parties, examining resource provision?

In developing such strategies, what has been the extent and nature of the involvement of

- teaching staff?
- outside professionals such as advisers?
- parents, managers?

Have experiences and developments been shared through

- statements and guidelines?
- group meetings?
- in-service work inside the school?
- in-service work outside the school?

Professional awareness

- Are staff aware of the language and dialect 'repertoires' of the pupils in the school?
- Do staff recognise that pupils' abilities to use language effectively have an important impact on their own view of themselves and therefore on their confidence as learners?
- Do they have a positive attitude to dialects other than standard? Is this reflected in the way they assess spoken and written language?
- Are staff knowledgeable about the mother tongues that their pupils speak, and do they see these as a potential or real strength in the school?

Pupils for whom English is a second language

Is there a system in the school for

- identifying pupils who need help with English as their second language?
- providing this help?
- monitoring the progress of pupils?

Are the teaching resources for English as a second language

- sufficient to meet the needs of the pupils in the school?
- available to pupils in a range of subjects?

Spoken language (all pupils)

Do the school's language policies result in the pupils

- developing confidence in approaching tasks that require a verbal response?
- speaking confidently to adult visitors?
- speaking clearly, so that they can be understood, irrespective of dialect or mother tongue?
- using a variety of words and phrases appropriate to their developmental age?
- using imagination to go beyond a given situation and introduce ideas of their own?

Attitudes to reading

Do the school's language policies result in the pupils
- expressing liking for, and enjoyment of, beginning reading processes?
- expressing liking for, and enjoyment of, later reading processes?

Introduction to reading

- Does the school use a reading scheme or schemes?
- How was it (were they) selected?
- What are the views of staff about the scheme(s) in use?
- What other supporting apparatus is used (e.g. pictures, games)?
- What other printed material is used?
- How are the reading materials utilised within the classroom:
    - (a) grouping of children for reading activities?
    - (b) are the instruction or learning situations formal or informal?
    - (c) is instruction with older pupils confined to children with specific reading difficulties?
    - (d) what is the usual time at which instruction sessions begin?
    - (e) what proportion of time is usually devoted to reading and supportive activities each day?
    - (f) what monitoring or record-keeping system is used?
    - (g) what would best describe the predominant approach to reading instruction in the school: look-and-say; phonics; a combination of the two; language experience?

Development of reading

- Is the school library centralised, a series of class libraries, a combination of both?
- Are parents involved in helping to organise it?
- Is the library well used by children?
- What do they read: comics, stories, information books, poetry?
- Do they like reading aloud in a group or by themselves?
- What actions does the school take to encourage children's interest in books (e.g. book club, visits to public library)?
- What actions are taken to extend reading to other subject areas?

(2) PARENTAL INVOLVEMENT IN READING

- Who initiated the reading involvement scheme?

- When was it launched?
- Were books sent home prior to the launching of the current scheme?
- If 'yes', what is different about the situation in the current project?

Selection of books to take home

Are the books chosen by

- the teacher (if 'yes', from a reading scheme/topic work/other)?
- the children?

If the children choose, do they have

- a limited range of books at a matched level?
- a wide range of books at various readability levels?
- books where the emphasis is on interest rather than reading level?

The home–school reading card

- Does the school use a reading card? If 'yes', has it been effective as a means of systematising parental involvement in children's reading development?
- How appropriate was this for families with little or no English?
- How was this problem overcome?
- Have other systems been used?

Workshops for parents

- Has the school run parent workshops? What form did they take?

Effects of the scheme

What have been the effects of the scheme

- on the children?
- on the parents?
- on the teachers?
- on language and reading policies in general?

What problems has the school experienced, and what steps have been taken to overcome them?

How has enthusiasm been maintained?

CHAPTER 9

Through the suspicion barrier

Ask the parents

The Coventry schools described in a previous chapter followed programmes involving parents that were, for the most part, sensitive and successful in reducing their sense of helplessness (in contrast to those analysed by Raven).[1] They had numerous, well-developed strategies for involving parents in their children's education, and especially in reading. The good results challenge the widely held pessimism about the effects of intervention programmes; they give support to simple, clear and easily replicated strategies that any local authority or school could adopt. Many schools all over Britain are following some of these programmes, but few local authorities have had consistent policies.[2]

What do schools do when they decide to embark on the course of involving parents, which so many teachers find perilous or threatening? It is always a good idea to ask the parents before formulating a view about their degree of interest in their children's education; there might be pleasant surprises! A questionnaire completed by fifty-three parents of nursery-age children in Salford showed that 69 per cent were willing to help in school; 92 per cent said they would like to borrow books from school, 56 per cent regularly; 60 per cent said they would like to see more activities for parents. Only 25 per cent gave an outright 'no'. Questions and comments parents added were about school holidays, meals, 'discipline' and the work the children would do in school, so that parents could better prepare them for it and help them with it. One respondent suggested that parents could watch the children during playtime and playground activities. Several commented on how helpful staff had been in giving information: 'I am very grateful to the teachers, who put everything they can into learning [*sic*] each child. It would be a good idea if in the few weeks before starting school the children could get to know the school and its teachers.'

Example: Woden Primary

Schools go about the job of easing parents through their doors in various ways, appropriate to the circumstances in which they operate. Woden Primary School was a 5–9-age-range school that had been open for five years. Children were accommodated in an open-plan building for 300, plus two large open-plan mobile units outside the main school block. The main catchment area of the school had been built between 4½ and 2½ years before I made my observations. It had predominantly young families, with a large proportion of free meals. The school had grown over this period to a number on roll of 361 children. There were eighteen teachers, plus the headteacher and part-time remedial help. The five first-year classes had between 23 and 25 children each; the other eleven classes had from 27 to 30 children each.

One teacher in the lower school and another in the middle school undertook group work with children with language and/or reading problems. They recorded their procedures as follows:

> We have encouraged parents to be involved in their children's education from the beginning, and parents are involved in the following ways throughout the school: (1) helping on a regular basis in school with activities like sewing and baking; (2) helping regularly on school educational visits, which are frequent; (3) helping with weekly library-book changing activities; (4) a great many parents attend our weekly children's assemblies, each Friday, when the children take the assembly; (5) a small number of parents help with fund-raising activities like jumble sales and spring fayres, as do a small number become involved in Harvest tea events, etc., which the school provides for the old people in the community; (6) second- and third-year parents have recently become involved in a home reading scheme.

The parent-and-toddler club was accommodated as follows:

(1) By re-arranging the PE timetable for two first-year classes on Tuesday afternoons, we have extended our Toy Loan Club to be in operation for the whole afternoon.

(2) Whilst they are in school, a teacher is allocated to keep an eye on the proceedings and on the success of the venture, intervening only when necessary with (a) advice on the activities offered and (b) encouragement to parents to mix socially with each other, if any seem shy or withdrawn. The parents work an informal rota system in looking after the register of parents/children attending each week and of the items borrowed from the toy/book loan stock; their willingness to accept responsibility increases all the time.

(3) The numbers attending the sessions have increased to an average of between twelve and eighteen children and parents present. A very informal atmosphere is developing partly due to the security offered by the supportive presence of one of the teachers in the lower school team. Even our probationary teacher is encouraged to take part (and supervise). The headteacher still pops in for at least ten or twenty minutes per session.

(4) Activities have been extended to include the following each week: sand/water play (very popular), painting, crayoning, cutting-out activities, plasticine modelling and sampling the toys available for loan before choosing.

Example: George Stephenson Primary

George Stephenson Primary School was a large open-plan school designed to accommodate 520 children in the 5–9-year-old age range. The building, which opened in September 1978, comprised six 'areas'. Each area consisted of an art/craft section, an open section, a semi-open section and a completely enclosed, carpeted 'quiet' room. A double mobile classroom was sited at the side of the playground.

The school had fifteen full-time primary teachers and 338 pupils on roll; the pupil–teacher ratio was 24:1. The number of pupils in each year varied considerably, but the number of 'rising fives' was expected to be between 70 and 75. The school also had a purpose-built forty-place nursery, staffed by two nursery teachers and two nursery assistants. As it was the only nursery on its council estate, the waiting-list contained about 150 names.

The headteacher provided this account:

Parental involvement has always been part of the nursery programme, and there has never been a shortage of volunteers for helping
in the nursery. Parents are involved in the primary school in the following ways:
Areas 1 and 2 (5–6-year-olds): taking small groups for number games,
language games and art/craft work; also for school outings.
Area 3 (6–7-year-olds): taking small groups for baking; also for school
outings.
Area 4 (7–8-year-olds): taking small groups for language and number
games and also baking; also for school outings.
　Parents frequently help with covering books and cards, repairing
equipment, making birthday cards, making concert costumes, dup-
licating work-sheets, etc. Many parents also help, in various ways,
with fund-raising events.

It soon became obvious that the nursery 'club' needed to expand,
both in scope and duration. In April 1983 it moved to a mobile
classroom and altered its time to 1.45–3.15 p.m. Extra activities
included the use of sand, clay, paint, chalk and Wendy house; story-
telling and simple handwork. Parents began to accept an increasing
amount of responsibility for organising the activities and for tea-
making. Although overall supervision by the teaching staff was
regarded as essential, there were occasions when it was impossible
for a teacher to be present for the first three-quarters of an hour, and
parents proved willing to run the club for this short period of time.
A gradual devolution of responsibility was favoured. The average
attendance was ten adults and up to twelve children. It soon became
possible to accommodate the club in a classroom in the main building. The area used had its own entrance and cloakroom facilities,
storage units and space for prams and pushchairs. Eventually the
headteacher took over a class to relieve a teacher to act as 'adviser' to
the group.

Example: St Dominic's Infants School

The headteacher's account:

First we tried inviting the parents to come into school in the morning
and afternoon instead of standing out in the street. Once they had
entered the building we encouraged them to help with coats and

shoes, and not just their own child's but any in need of help, and to supervise until the bell rang for prayers. Then they were invited to join in morning prayers. The results were initial delight and tremendous participation. The children were definitely happier – no tears or tantrums any more – and parents are finding it easier to talk with staff, often discussing problems not relating to the child or school.

A rota for helping in school was worked out, as so many parents were keen to come. This year, however,

the novelty may have worn off, as only three mums have asked to help. Help with cookery was not very successful at first but much better when the mother had helped the teacher with a group to get the idea of using language while working. Working with sewing has been very successful and means the children don't have to queue for help. Not all mothers can manage reading stories, and cassette stories are useful here. Some still seem apprehensive of the older teachers as if recollecting their own school days, but there is a noticeable change in attitude to staff and school after a few visits. Not one parent has ever interferred with or criticised teachers' work methods.

We hold parents' evenings for new mothers with each new intake, discuss how we teach the 'three Rs' etc., and the parents can try out the apparatus used by the children. This is always well attended. At half-term parents come from 2 to 8 p.m., to talk about their children's progress. There are also PTA social evenings, dances and car rallies. Many new friendships are formed, but always there are the same fifty parents – never the ones we really need to meet. However well attended these meetings are, the half-dozen parents we need to see never attend. These I visit, but there isn't much response.

I feel we have so far merely scratched the surface. We must try harder to canvass the idea of parent participation and try to give more time to showing parents what to do when they come into school. Some show no initiative whatsoever; some seem natural helpers. Others would enjoy coming but they are tied up with young babies or are employed outside the home. I have yet to find a way to interest some mothers in their child's education, and some still regard us as a dumping ground from 9.00 to 3.30 or often 4.30 when they forget to collect the child. Fortunately these are only a few.

Something we still have to try is grandparent participation. In this area the young working mothers receive a great deal of support from their own mothers. The children spend much time with their grandparents; and so the over-sixties club secretary has been contacted, and notices will be read out in church.

Example: Hazel Primary

An inner-city school that appears to have broken through most of the traditional barriers is Hazel Primary School and Community Centre in Leicester, opened in December 1982 and awarded a Schools Curriculum Award in 1984. It was the first centre of its kind within the city, providing facilities for those living in the Tower and Walnut Street areas and the St Andrew's estate. Local residents were instrumental in obtaining the facilities, and much of the work relies on the goodwill and enthusiasm of the local people. The then head-teacher (Pat Clark) was also warden of the community centre. Combining these two roles requires the exercise of many varied skills. On one occasion I found her preparing lunch for the senior citizens' club, assisted by three of her pupils (two boys and a girl). She talked about curriculum development while breaking eggs to make a sponge-cake, mentioning the psychologist Bruner and the psycho-linguist Gordon Wells while paying tribute to the television cook Delia Smith – a performance of real virtuosity!

What struck me was the *combination* of a good primary school catering for the needs of children living in a very disadvantaged area of the city, with an active community centre. Among courses offered were wine-making, old-time dancing, French, Indian cooking and Caribbean cooking. These courses were available to unemployed people at a 75 per cent reduction in fees. Both the centre and the school issued brochures, describing their courses and curriculum; and a regular newsletter, *The Walnut Grapevine*, combined school and community news, using appropriate community languages. Most of the functions of school brochures listed by Bastiani were to be found in these publications – see Figure 9.1.[4]

Reading project at Dean's Lane Infants

The following account was written for me by the staff of this delightful school.

> We all agree that we want parents involved in their child's reading. This project, called Reading Together, had been in operation for a little over two terms at the time of observation. Before embarking on

Figure 9.1 Some functions of school brochures

Basic information model • Makes necessary information available. • Concern for organisational efficiency.	*Public relations model* • Projects a positive image of the life and work of the school (distinct sub-types).
Parental involvement model Encourages parents to become actively involved in • the education of their children; • the life and work of the school.	*Development model* • Provides information and support during the process of entry/transfer.

the project it was decided that each teacher should organise her own Reading Together rather than adopt a uniform approach because:

(1) We were trying something new – it would involve trial and error. We didn't want to be restricted by too rigid a plan.

(2) We could take advantage of a wide variety of approaches when dealing with problems. We could draw on each other's experiences.

(3) Each of us has our own particular way of organising reading in our classrooms, and the project would need to fit in with that.

(4) Each of us had our own preferences for which group we wanted to start first and the number of children we wanted to be involved.

(5) No two classes were the same. There were classes of 'top'-year children; some 'top'-year and some middle-year children. All the children in the class were involved.

This variety was reflected in the arrangements for taking books home. One class took them away every night (with no adverse comment if the book was not read); another three times a week (if the child chose to); another allowed the child free choice. Children chose books from the same range that was read with the teachers. When the book was read at home, it was read again with the teacher *only* if the child wanted to.

Record-keeping systems also varied. (1) The teachers and parent(s) shared the same book to record the child's reading. (2) Teachers kept a separate record of the child's reading in school but commented on the Reading Together booklet when appropriate. The parent(s) recorded their child's reading in this booklet and wrote a comment if they wished.

All the staff were enthusiastic, despite

(a) Having to compromise with our plans – we couldn't always get the group we wanted and had to settle for those who were prepared to get involved. So much for precision planning.

(b) Too much enthusiasm – some children wanted to be involved before the teacher was ready. The teacher just had to speed up her plans.

(c) Teething troubles – one of use needed to try different styles of booklet before she found the one she liked.

(d) Failures – there are some parents we have not been able to sell the idea to, but we are reluctant to accept the 'you can't win 'em all' theory.

Example: Sutton Centre

Although there are very few examples, secondary schols can also be found where parental participation is more than a gleam in the head-teacher's eye.

Sutton Centre in Nottinghamshire, opened in 1973, has been one of the most discussed community schools in the country. It has been, to my knowledge, the only school to accept a resident research officer. Fletcher has produced a vivid and detailed account of the school's trials and triumphs during its formative years, concluding that Sutton Centre's success was in 'simultaneously standing for progressive education; inter-professional co-operation; practical public welfare; and sensible use of public property'.[5]

Less well-known were the sustained and successful efforts made to contact parents through home visits or at the Centre. In the early 1980s I was asked to analyse a questionnaire completed by staff and to discuss the results with them at a one-day conference. At that time (and this probably remains true) the staff were virtually unanimous about the value of close links between home and school and especially of the initial home visit, which enabled them to assert that contact was made with 100 per cent of parents and not just the usual 15 to 25 per cent of supportive, open-evening/social-attending parents.

Teachers found home visiting or meeting parents to be of value for many reasons:

- Sorting out behaviour problems.
- Getting to know home environment and parents.
- Hearing more about pupils (sometimes confidential).
- Discovering that pupils actually tell their parents very little about school, work or events taking place in the Centre. (They were able to supply this information to parents and also to dispel misleading rumours often heard about the Centre.)
- Parents' support for school was more forthcoming.
- Sometimes parents were able to inform the tutor about problems their child had that were not obvious in school (medical/social/emotional).
- Seeing the home environment made tutors more aware and better equipped to cope with problems.
- Explaining the basic philosophy of Sutton Centre, about courses, feedback from profiles, etc. ('Easier for them to express concern about their child's progress; they would not have taken the trouble to come into school over some of the minor points.')

One teacher summarised the effects:

Meeting parents is of tremendous importance. If you live in the community you are more likely to build up a good relationship with your parents through incidental meetings. They start to confide in you more if you meet them regularly. You become a 'friend', not just a teacher of their child, if they are able to ring you up at home with any worries they may have, knowing you care enough to sort them out as best you can, after the initial first-year home visit. The initial home visit helps to give them confidence when the need arises to ask questions or discuss worries.

Another member of staff put the advantages in these terms:

- Parents felt far more relaxed and confident about discussing their problems and worries, particularly when they knew they could ring their child's tutor up at home and have a chat informally.
- Parents find it more satisfying to be on friendly, informal terms with the tutor.

- Parents were pleased to learn that the school was a good place, with concerned and competent staff. The home visit allowed them to assess and get to know the tutor, so that they gained the confidence to contact the school.

The head and staff gave very careful consideration to these home visits – as well they might when every teacher, including probationers, was expected to take part. A briefing document, offering down-to-earth advice, was prepared and discussed.

> Home visiting is a two-edge sword. Teachers are seen with their guards down, off-duty, out of the ivory tower, all of which true educationalists may well applaud; but not many parents expect teachers to be . . . always be, and particularly on home visits, highly professional.

This kind of straight talk was necessary when a whole staff was expected to undertake visits. It is an entirely different concept of home–school liaison. The HSLT has usually been expected to have special qualities, best exercised by a trained, dedicated teacher or worker – as in the following example, a study of a home–school liaison office in a residential school for maladjusted children.

Elm Hill Special School

Elm Hill School accepted emotionally disturbed boys and girls aged 9–16. The premises were purpose-built in 1976 to cater for 30 boarders – 19 boys and 19 girls – and 12 day pupils. Most of the pupils came from Southshire, and a few from Northshire, having been sent 'out county' by the education authority. At first the school was fully residential, but then it was closed every other weekend, all the children becoming fortnightly or weekly boarders, or day pupils. Transport home was provided for all pupils every other weekend and for children in Southshire who wished to go home daily or weekly. Other pupils wishing to go home more frequently had to make their own arrangements; a number used public transport to go home for weekends. The school was situated on the outskirts of a market town in a quiet residential area. Public transport to the school was possible, though infrequent and time-consuming.

The headteacher had been with the school since it opened, and the deputy nearly as long. Apart from these two there were six teachers, giving an approximate pupil–teacher ratio of 8:1 at most times. Five child-care staff performed the majority of morning, evening and weekend duties with assistance from some teachers in performing extraneous duties. This meant five staff on duty most evenings, giving an approximate ratio of 7:1. There tended to be a regular turnover of staff in the school, so that in-service training and support were a continuous process.

The school was run on democratic principles as far as possible, with staff given much of the responsibility for everyday decisions. The head and deputy shared the overall responsibility to a great extent, avoiding a hierarchical structure in the staffing. As one or other of these was on duty every working night and weekend, immediate decisions could be taken in times of difficulty or crisis, allowing prompt action.

Children were referred to the school for a wide variety of reasons, which were listed under seven headings, with many children presenting more than one problem: severe temper tantrums/aggression; disobedient/disruptive behaviour; dangerous/bizarre behaviour; gross attention-seeking in other ways; stealing; non-attendance/school refusal; nervous, withdrawn. The recent trend has been towards an increase in acting-out children with behaviour problems being admitted to the school. Most of the children recommended for placement at Elm Hill were those that pose the greatest problem to mainstream education. The head summarised that 'the average Elm Hill child entering at present is likely to be a twelve-plus aggressive, disruptive, disobedient city-born boy, suspended from school, with an IQ of 89, but three years retarded in basics'. Most were considered to be emotionally disturbed. Many would have a deep mistrust of all adults, particularly those in authority; many would have very low self-esteem, having received negative messages from schools and from their parents. A high percentage of the children came from 'broken homes'; half were currently living in one-parent families or with step-parents. Many had had to cope with (and were still having to cope with) violence, death or illness in their homes.

Although the primary aim of the school was to educate the children effectively and efficiently, this could not be done unless there was trust, security and stability in the school. The staff therefore had a therapeutic role to play as well as an educational one. Here, perhaps more than in any other type of school, the emotional and social needs of the children had to be considered.

Why a home–school liaison officer?

The headmaster and the deputy head had worked closely together at the school and both felt that there was a need for closer contact between the parents and the school. For many of the children the family was a major or exacerbating factor in the aetiology of their maladjustment. The emotional and practical difficulties in their homes may have placed them under considerable stress, and for most it was thought to be beneficial for them to have a residential educational placement, at least for a while. However, all the children went home on alternate weekends, some every weekend and a few every day. After home visits, or after contacts with their families at other times, the children were often upset, angry or worried, and their behaviour reflected their feelings. They might become more disruptive or more withdrawn; but in either case their ability to attend and learn in class was reduced, and the stability of the whole class was upset. In these situations it was difficult for the school to educate the children effectively. It was thus essential that the staff were aware of each child's family situation and were kept informed of changing circumstances.

The head and the deputy had long been committed to establishing and maintaining good relationships with parents. Great attention was paid to the initial interview, when it was stressed that the school was willing to help, and could be contacted at any time. Parents interviewed had all found the school friendly and helpful at their initial meeting, and none felt any hesitation in contacting the school if they were worried or needed advice. As few families had transport of their own, and most lived some distance from the school, contact with the school was largely by telephone. Parents found the school approachable and available: 'I can always pick up the phone whenever I'm worried. I'm happy in my own mind that I can find out whatever I want to'; 'I can always get in touch with them. It doesn't matter what time of day or night, they'll always talk to you.'

Similarly, if the school had a problem it would usually get in touch with parents by telephone or letter. Only one parent interviewed felt that the school did not keep her informed well in this way. However, contact from the school usually indicated that there was a problem concerning the child. Only in instances of acute crisis or difficulty did staff from the school visit families in their homes. The staffing in school, the need for constantly high staff-to-child ratios and the distances to be travelled made such visits difficult, and they were undertaken only rarely. The fact that very few of the care staff had a driver's licence exacerbated this problem.

For several years the education welfare service allocated responsibility to one educational welfare officer (EWO) who worked fairly closely with the school, bringing families to the school for their initial interview and maintaining some contact with them afterwards. The service was subsequently reorganised, and special-school pupils became the responsibility of the EWO working with the referring school. The head at Elm Hill found that he might be dealing with a different EWO for each child in his school, none of whom could be expected to know his school well, and who had not got the time to continue the work of the previous officer. The contact between Elm Hill and the pupils' homes therefore diminished.

The school staff found that where they had previously been working with a minimum amount of information about the families and some liaison support from outside, they were now without either. They said that it was difficult teaching children whom they knew little about, particularly if the situations at home were changing, when they had no time to get the information they required, and no one they could ask to get it for them. All of the staff spoke of the difficulties during this year. The situation in the school deteriorated. The headteacher, aware that the additional expense to the LEA would be the main stumbling-block, particularly at a time when government cut-backs were beginning to bite, explored ways of creating a new post without much extra cost. The difficulties were discussed at length with all the school staff, who agreed that it might be worth reorganising the school to allow the creation of such a post, as the need for a home–school liaison worker was so great.

The school had up until this time been open every weekend for termly boarders. It was suggested that if it closed on alternate weekends, making the school a 'fortnightly' boarder, fewer care staff would be needed, and one houseparent post could be reallocated as an HSL officer post. Fortunately, one of the houseparents was leaving at the end of the summer term, allowing the reorganisation to take place; the remaining care staff agreed to work longer consecutive hours in a new timetable.

The education authority was sympathetic to the needs of the school. It saw the reorganisation of the timetable to a fortnightly rather than a termly boarding establishment as an opportunity to create a new post of HSL officer, responsible to the headteacher, who was in turn accountable to the school governors and to the LEA. The job description sent out to applicants for the post listed the following roles:

> Make contact with the family prior to the child's entry to the school, to prepare the child and the family for entry to a special school, and all the attendant difficulties, mundane and emotional which this might present.
>
> During the child's school life act as a bridge between home and school. During the pupil's school life some families require fairly constant or frequent contact and help, whilst others need less active intervention. Contact should be maintained even with those families who are not making constant demands for attention and to ensure that reciprocal awareness of school and family conditions and feelings is brought about.
>
> Some of the time will be spent in school at staff meetings, gathering information from various sources within the school and meeting the children within the school setting.
>
> Maintaining links between home, school and other agencies. Liaison with the Child and Family Psychiatric Service, Social Services, DHSS and Education Welfare will be a useful ingredient.
>
> Towards the end of a pupil's stay at school, the Liaison Officer could be of great help to the Careers Service and the Careers Teacher in helping to seek appropriate employment and even some after-care,

The successful candidate was an education welfare officer who had been responsible for all the special schools, including Elm Hill. She therefore had the advantage of knowing many of the children and the staff in the school. She also knew other professionals in the area, some of whom would be useful contacts in the new post.

Before she began the job, the HSL officer drew up a statement of intent, detailing the duties she thought she should fulfil. These were, in brief: social-work support to pupils on roll, families of pupils, school staff; updating data on pupils and maintaining case files; professional contact with prepared formal links, i.e. EWO service, schools psychological service, social services, assessment and observation centres, child and family psychiatric service, the juvenile liaison officers, school medical officer and specialist careers officer; member of multi-disciplinary admission and review panels. The HSL officer thus had a clear conception of the areas of work the new post entailed. The roles she listed reflected her experience as an education welfare officer, with an awareness of the importance of a professional approach to the job, and of recording information.

Many of the staff, including the headteacher, thought that it was important to employ a non-teacher for the post. First, they said teachers do not generally have experience or training in counselling or social work, and often find it difficult to relate to parents. Secondly, it was important that the HSL officer should not be identified as a member of the teaching staff, since she should maintain a neutral role within the school, being trusted equally by staff and parents. The post-holder was well aware of the need to take a neutral role in the school. In her notes on the 'outlines of duties to be undertaken' she wrote:

> I feel strongly that it must be an autonomous post. Although being on the school staff, parents must see that you are impartial, being able to trust you and your judgements to be unbiased. In reverse, the school staff must not see you as identifying with the parents. The pupils must be your primary concern; therefore the approach you use with them is even more important, to gain their confidence . . . the pupils should not see too much liaison with school staff, headmaster and parents.

This special school for maladjusted children has been described in some detail because close contact with the home is exceptionally difficult to maintain when the school is residential. It illustrated the (perhaps unnecessary) limitations of this form of residential provision but also demonstrates the capacity of professional staff to overcome them. It should also be noted that the decision to redistribute the burden of teaching and supervision was taken by the staff as a whole. An education welfare officer was appointed to the post; and so, in this instance at least, more than lip-service was paid to the need for closer co-operation between teachers and the other caring professions.

Home and school involvement in Salford and Leicester

I was asked to evaluate a two-year project (1983–5) set up by the Community Education Development Centre in conjunction with two local education authorities, Salford and Leicester. The project generated plenty of activities, and in a few schools began to bring about lasting changes in the direction of the teachers' interests. A full account of this project is available.[6] I would like to draw attention to aspects that were unusual and are likely to be of general interest.

Management

The lot of the innovator is likely to be a hard one, whatever precautions are taken in advance, but the project staff came to be regarded as useful and conscientious workers whose presence in schools was welcome. Both authorities at the time of writing (1985) had renewed the secondment of the project staff and had given indications that the project would continue. Even in retrospect, it is not easy to identify specific ways in which they could have been better managed because so many events were outside the control of any individual or group of individuals. A capacity for expecting the unexpected appears an essential quality in successful project management.

Starting-up strategies

The following activities were initiated in one school in the first term by the project leader.

- A weekly drop-in, a social activity where mothers could meet together and enjoy a cup of tea and a chat. Some brought their children, and sometimes there were three generations present. Teachers were encouraged to drop in and have their afternoon tea with the parents.
- Toy library.
- Book library.
- Ready-for-school group, meeting weekly. Parents whose children were coming into the school were invited to attend a series of meetings where the children had a chance to work in the nursery and the head and staff were able to talk to the parents about the school.
- Curriculum workshops, designed to explain a particular curriculum area.
- Pre-school reading programme, enabling parents to come weekly to borrow early-reading and picture books for their children. Advice and encouragement were provided by teaching staff, and discussion of children's books was encouraged.
- Identifying needs of the individual mother and child led to a programme devised as a concentrated daily boost in language and reading skills. One (Indian) mother and child were taught

conversational English through games; another (English) mother and child were similarly taught reading together. This led to:

- The paired reading programme (as descibed in Chapter 8) being introduced in the lower junior school. Again, this programme was used as a concentrated boost with children who were a little way below their reading age. The programme lasted for five weeks and involved two home visits by teachers and one group meeting of parents in school.
- a parent/community association meeting was held to discuss its role and objectives. Out of this grew:
- the after-school care programme and
- Holiday play-schemes.
- Home visiting was put into practice by both nursery staff and reading teachers.
- A gift of a small starter-pack of educational materials proved a useful device for ice-breaking and a focus for discussion. They were used both when visiting and at ready-for-school groups.
- A special event was organised and run by the parents to raise money for a playground.
- Teacher-directed classroom activities in which parents partici- pated had been going on for some time. Parents came to help with cooking and sewing, etc. Some parents had skills to offer beyond this; for instance, they were encouraged to come and tell stories in their mother tongue, to help with dances at festivals and generally to look again at their own skills that they had not fully recognised.
- Parent librarians were trained to help in the school library.
- Gujarati lessons were offered to teachers.

Contacts with other agencies

Both the Salford and Leicester projects made efforts to involve agen- cies other than the education service, and a good web of contacts was established, as we have seen. In the first few months, the Leicester team was in touch with LITS (the language, interpreting and trans- lating service), the Health Education Council and the local library. Both teams worked closely with various under-fives organisations. In Leicester a determined, early effort was made to establish an adventure playground; a parents' meeting was called early in November 1983, attended by two staff and five parents; everyone chipped in with offers of materials, contacts and know-how. The library service proved particularly supportive. In April 1984 five 'librarian mums' went to the (Services to Education) library, where they watched a video, chatted with the librarian and bought books. On that occasion the first books in Gujarati were chosen for one school library.

Another agency that has been consistently supportive in both authorities has been the health service, usually in the person of the health visitors, who have spoken to numerous parent-and-child groups. The search for contacts outside the education service has been continuous, as may be seen from the records for 1984–5, during which the project leaders met representatives from (among others) a community centre, a recreation centre, WEA *re* a health course, community health visitors (two visits), a Law Centre, the local baths, a health visitor, a National Children's Bureau survey, the Urban Policies subcommittee (*re* pre-school equipment), Loughborough University (student involvement), Community Relations Commission.

These contacts, though inspiring to the project staff and the women's groups, did not make as much impact on school staff as was hoped, mainly perhaps because of lack of time. Those teachers who were contacted by, for example, health visitors were invariably keen and wanted more.

Home visiting

Teachers making their first home visits to Asian families ensured that there was someone within the family group who could provide communication. One enthusiastic teacher felt that these cautious opening gambits had enabled him to establish his strengths and weaknesses, and he had soon widened his visits to include most parents in his classes. The reading teacher who initiated the scheme was well pleased although, as she put it, she had had 'to lead many teachers by the hand to parental homes'. Home visiting was also undertaken by the head of a nursery unit for children about to enter the nursery. On each occasion, she took the project's ready-for-school pack; it was received with pleasure and adequately occupied each child. Mothers were able to talk about their concerns, and she could reassure them on several points.

One class teacher cut through the objections that were raised about visiting parents in their homes by arranging to go home with one child each evening until all had been visited. Most of the children lived within easy walking distance, it is true, but the same would apply to many other schools that seem to find the difficulties of home visiting insuperable.

Pre-school children: parent-and-child groups

An outstanding example of a parent-and-toddler group was observed at Norton Infants School in 1983. It was virtually autonomous, under the control of the parents themselves, who set up the apparatus and organised the group in the large central hall. The headteacher maintained a discreet background presence. One of the mothers led the group, mainly by example. Two fathers were present. All the children and parents were occupied; there was a hum of purposeful activity; coffee came round; children changed from one set of apparatus to another without disruption; spontaneous discussion groups formed, including (or not including) members of the school staff.

This group was still very strong in March 1985, despite a period of some difficulty, according to the project leader:

> The parent-and-toddler group has regained its former numbers with about 30 on register and 18–19 regular attenders, now that it has moved back to the original Tuesday morning spot. The nursery teacher, who is very interested in parental involvement, has been getting to know the children and parents in the group. She is keen to set up a 'share a story' session next term and also to lend out equipment as there is no toy library. I have made simple number and matching games to start the scheme off.
>
> The nursery teacher in an adjacent classroom pops in and out and circulates amongst the parents. She is obviously very interested in increasing the contact between her class and the toddlers' group and will be a valuable link in the development of work here.
>
> My only regret again is that the group cannot meet more than once a week because of lack of available hall space. Also, because there are now thirty on the register, Mrs W. is wondering if she is soon going to have to start putting people on the waiting-list.

In another Salford school, a similar pattern was established (reported in autumn 1983):

On 7 March we opened the toddler group. This is run every Wednesday morning, 9 to 11 o'clock, by the mums as I am not available. Two mothers are in charge, though I have stressed the aim is to involve everyone in organising and helping in the group. The group is for parents, babies, toddlers up to school age. Some of the children who come to the Thursday group come to this group too. The children are already showing signs of being at home in the school. Parents have noticed their children being more sociable and able to relate to other adults. The group has thirteen children on its register and is advertised through posters in school and mentions in the newsletter. Parents who come to put their child's name down for school are also told about the group.

Toddler group training sessions' were occasionally held, with parents being invited from other schools:

The parents found the talk on language especially valuable and they also enjoyed the art workshop. We showed them ideas with paint to use at the toddler group, e.g. straw-blowing, string prints, printing with shapes and sponges, bubble prints and folded paper prints. All the mothers had a go; so did the children and they thoroughly enjoyed themselves. A few now comment on how much more they know and understand about school – what we do and why we do it. They are all keen to help their children at home.

Book libraries were established in several schools, some run by the parents themselves.

Toy libraries

A questionnaire to parents revealed a surprising reluctance to make use of a toy library, in contrast to their eager support of book libraries and offers of help in many other ways. The head of a nursery in Salford had some reservations herself, wondering if their best use might be for demonstrating to mothers what to buy (say, for Christmas) and noting that some parents feel threatened by offers of toys and react defensively. Even so, a substantial toy library had been established here, and a group of registered child-minders met regularly at the nursery, examining the toys and discussing their possible uses in their own situations – a perhaps unexpected example of the 'ripple effects' sought by the project.

Elsewhere in Salford, toy libraries were used with variable enthusiasm, as this 1983 project leader's report shows:

The toy library was opened on Thursday 8 March. It is open during the ready-for-school group, so parents of pre-school children attending the group may borrow toys. It is also open on a Friday morning for parents of children in the nursery and reception classes. There is a great response from the Thursday group, with most parents borrowing a toy every week. The response is small on a Friday, only four parents, but at present the toys are not a wide enough range to cater for all the children. Disappointing is the lack of use of the jigsaws. The most popular toys are Duplo Lego, Sticklebricks, train set, threading animal shapes, picture dominoes, tea-set. We need more picture-matching games to extend those children ready for school. Toys most noticeably not used; cotton reels and threads, language pictures, wooden construction animals, scissors, telephone.

The caution with which some mothers approach toy libraries is understandable. They are worried about breakages or losses and require reassuring. Once this was achieved, they borrowed readily, as the records in Salford and Leicester revealed. The latter team achieved a notable sucess, in that its application to the National Toy Library Association was approved, bring both a grant of money to supplement its library and the accolade of recognition. Some of its apparatus was self-made, the rest carefully chosen from catalogues, and it was all meticulously arranged in packs with written suggestions for possible use in English and Gujarati. There was a wide range of jigsaws, dominoes, snap lock beads, lotto, snap cards and other language games. Providing suggestions for activities in the mother tongue has been a successful ploy. The toys came and went frequently, and were equally popular among Asian and white mothers. The system of putting the small items into self-contained packs may have had a bearing on the mothers' willingness to borrow. It was encouraging that the mothers' initial misgivings could be overcome so effectively.

Drop-in groups

Both projects were eager to welcome parents to social gatherings and discussion groups. High Moor School's 'drop-in' group held eighteen Friday afternoon sessions between October 1983 and March 1984. There was a total of 41 people on the register, of whom 13 joined in the first three weeks and 7 in the last three. The average attendance was 10, with the largest session attracting 18 and the smallest 3. One mother attended 17 out of 18; six attended more than 50 per cent. Nine parents came once only, and it would be interesting to know what their expectations were, and whether these were satisfied by a single visit. In general, the project leader had every reason to feel pleased: 'It is very successful, with a core of regulars who did not know one another before, and new members arriving each week.'

Both there and at Ashley Infants, the project staff found it difficult to attract and retain support from the regular school staff. They found themselves doing most of the work themselves, except when specific talks by staff members were requested.

At Adenfield School, it was known as the 'coffee group'. According to the project leader:

> The year started with some new members plus the usual regulars. Parents of children who have moved into the juniors still show an interest. There have been problems within the group – a disagreement over the form their Christmas play should take, and the 'rowdiness' of certain mums putting other mums off coming to the group. This has been partly solved by forming a Quiet Group. However I still feel there are a lot mums we are not reaching.
>
> We have had good attendance when outside speakers have come to talk to the group (Safety in the Home, Dental Hygiene). Group numbers range between 10 and 16 parents.
>
> The Keep Fit moved to a Wednesday so that mums could use the hall. Unfortunately there has been a decline in the number of mums wanting to take part (2–3 mums), and the instructor is starting full-time work in November. I had tried to persuade a mum to take the group, but no one thought it worthwhile for only two of them so the group was closed. I have tried to encourage more attendance by (1) putting up posters throughout the school; (2) telling parents I met; it's amazing how many parents say afterwards that they didn't know anything about the talks.

Open University child development courses

Nine mothers agreed to take sponsored places on experimental Open University courses in child development. One withdrew immediately she received the materials (comprising eight books, two to each pack), feeling the demands of the course were too great. It is probable in retrospect that she could have been encouraged to make a start if the materials had been presented differently and, if so, she might have managed as well as the others, several of whom said how apprehensive they were at first, but found that these feelings diminished as the course proceeded. Among other features, they found that there was no obligation to complete the 'tests' but in the event they all wanted to do so:

> One of 'my' mums has completed the OU course, The Pre-School Child, and passed all four assignments. She was thrilled to bits – she is a parent who is always running herself down. So we made quite a fuss of her. I felt exhilarated myself, as though I had achieved something. I am throwing a surprise celebration for her on the last day of term.

They were all enthusiastic and had enjoyed the challenge. They considered that their knowledge of children's development had been enhanced and their powers of observation enlarged: 'It's what we do automatically, but the course makes you think about what you do.' There had been considerable disagreement over the parts of the course that made specific suggestions for allowing children to undertake tasks. They all saw the point and had reviewed their supervision policies, but still considered that the course presenter had the wrong emphasis; it was all right for the children to make a sandwich, even though this might result in messy play, but cutting with a sharp knife was too dangerous for this age group (2–5 years). There was general comment about the concept-acquisition tasks, which revealed children's learning processes in unexpected ways.

At least two of the mothers intended to take the course for the next age range. Their participation in the Open University course, they felt, had improved the quality of the mother-and-toddler groups by generating informed discussion and creating fresh interest, even when it proceeded from disagreement. The course could be ranked as successful in its main aims of stimulating this kind of interest and, it seemed, of whetting the appetite of most of the mothers for 'education'. Considerable interest was expressed in continuing these studies during the next phase of the project.

Were the project's aims achieved?

The project's initiatives were not confined within the 'communications' (or 'busy-work') model but, in numerous instances, achieved

(1) Home–school	(2) Pre-school	(3) Children out of school
e.g. • Parental involvement in reading, mathematics, family curriculum; home visiting • Drop-in groups, family clubs, films, PTA	e.g. • Home visiting of next years' pupils • Ready-for-school groups • Mother-and-toddler groups • Links with local play-groups	e.g. • Out-of-school activities • Holiday play scheme • Latchkey programme
(a) Curriculum		
(b) Social events		

(4) School reflected in the community	(5) Community reflected in the school	(6) Adult education
e.g. • Work displayed at local sites • Community service work by children • Newsletter	e.g. • Curriculum includes local studies • Reference material on locality • Local people offer skills and memories • Agencies outside the education service involved	e.g. • At least one class on offer • Self-help groups • Links with local community college
		(a) Education for personal and social development
		(b) Education related particularly to role as parent

Figure 9.2   Community education development schedule: monthly summary of school's parental contacts

genuine co-operation in organising new styles of learning through parental involvement.

- Webs of contacts were established, involving many agencies both within and outside the education service.
- Examples of effective practice were demonstrated and generalised. The prospects for the continuation of this work were, at the time of writing, reasonably good in both authorities.
- Contacts with teacher training institutions were productive. Students have worked in Salford schools, where they have been warmly welcomed and have learned some of the realities of classroom work with adults.
- Work with pre-school children and their parents was in process in fourteen schools, with parents exercising 'controlled autonomy' in some of them.
- Reading and language development programmes with associated home visiting were well established in at least four schools and could be viewed as breaking new ground in three of them.

Considering the very difficult circumstances obtaining in the schools during the two years of the project, these achievements were a fair response to the aims set out at the beginning.

This chapter has been devoted to success stories in involving parents. It is not claimed that there are many examples of genuine participation, particularly in secondary schools, but it has been shown that all the essential groundwork had been done over and over again; the process has been described for others to follow if they will – Figure 9.2 suggests a matrix for recording home–school contacts. The next chapter continues on the same theme, describing an authentic case of full-scale parental participation.

CHAPTER 10

Collaborative learning: small is beautiful

Neighbourhood Centre Project, North Humberside

McMillan Nursery School was purpose-built in 1939 and has three large rooms connected by a long corridor. It is situated in the middle of the North Hull council estate, though its catchment area also includes a few pockets of private housing. The Neighbourhood Centre Project, based in the nursery school, has provided one of the few recorded examples of the exercise of parental autonomy in a British school. It was originated and sustained by Margaret Rice, who with her co-director Patrick Doyle has written substantively about the project.[1] I had the great pleasure of spending time in Humberside, staying overnight with parents on the estate and joining the activity groups to view work in progress and completed.

The nursery school itself was a joy. The atmosphere was notably warm and welcome. All members of staff were included in a team effort to involve parents and to convey this operationally through conversation, provision of facilities, displays of children's work and in other ways. The headteacher was able to develop control by democratic means, and many members of staff expressed their satisfaction at being 'included' in decision-making. A newly appointed ancillary contrasted the friendly atmosphere and attitude of staff with her experience at her previous school. Parents attended Christmas concerts with the greatest enthusiasm – virtually all of the mothers and a good number of fathers. The many problems encountered by the parents certainly did not prevent them from turning out on these occasions; the concerts were joyous and informal, with many opportunities for participation. There was also a constant stream of parents coming and going, some calling on the head. An observer could not fail to note that this school valued parental contacts and had created an organisational structure allowing for them to occur without disruption to the routine of a good nursery school.

A head start?

The classes observed were all taught by qualified nursery teachers with nursery nurses, giving a reasonable pupil–staff ratio. The staff were well-informed about individual children's needs, and made efforts to provide varied treatment for them during the course of a day's programme. The development of language skills was encouraged through individual conversation and small group work. Wall displays of children's work, posters and teachers' project work produced a colourful and stimulating learning environment. The social, physical and emotional needs were evidently very well catered for.

Two aspects of the staff's behaviour, which have already been identified as predominating at the McMillan nursery, are closely associated with the achievements of children: teacher enthusiasm and warmth. 'These behaviours not only elicit greater response from each individual but also create for the whole class a climate of involvement reflected in the attitudes of pupils to each other, to the teacher and to learning.'[2]

The effects of a 'head start' have been fully documented in the massive volume by Zigler and Valentine, which established that there were significant long-term differences between the Head Start children and others (see Chapter 2). In summary, 'the data from these studies appears to be compelling evidence for the effects of early childhood education, especially on those variables which best measure the ability to survive in the schools'.[3] 'Over the years, parents of Head Start youngsters have consistently maintained that the programme has done remarkable things for their children and themselves.'[4]

Pre-schooling plus parent education

Whether 'traditional' nursery education as practised in Britain delivers the benefits discerned by the Head Start evaluations has been questioned. The combination of pre-schooling and parent education has been identified as the key factor. Professionally organised nurseries tend to involve parents, if at all, on their own terms. Several studies – by Bruner,[5] Tizard,[6] Tizard, Mortimore and Burchell,[7] and Smith[8] – look analytically at parental involvement in nursery schools and classes and compare it with the spin-off in terms of parental self-confidence generated by pre-school play-groups. All these studies revealed that after a decade of talking about involvement there was in the late 1970s and early 1980s very little to show in the way of *participation* in the education process, as opposed to helping on the periphery, although attitudes amongst professionals were generally favourable. A similar picture in primary schools was confirmed in the research by Cyster and others.[9] By contrast the Pre-School Playgroups' Association at its annual conference in 1983 specifically changed its aims from providing play opportunities for young children to 'encouraging parents to understand and provide for the needs of their children under statutory age through community groups'.

In this context it can be seen that McMillan Nursery School has been creating a style of relationship with parents that is still comparatively unusual in Britain. 'Parents have been provided with the opportunity to talk, to be listened to and to share a problem': this statement was certainly in accord with what I observed there. The school was operating within a web of carefully fostered links with the social services, the health authority and the NSPCC, and with the neighbouring primary, junior high and senior high schools (older girls come in to play with the nursery children once a week). There was a library session at which the children with a parent were encouraged to take a book home, and where parents helped to organise the distribution of books. A newsletter was sent to parents once a month to inform them of general activities. Staff and parents have worked together to raise funds and on transforming part of the school garden into a safe and attractive landscaped area with shrubs, trees and flowers.

Informal contacts with parents, already mentioned, were actively promoted by the staff creating a parents' room where 'pop-in' sessions were established in January 1982. Parents, including a grandfather, came in frequently for these sessions. A large number of the children had speech and language problems; some adults had depressive and other psychological conditions; and there were many one-parent families, including some with imprisoned fathers. The staff's response of developing activities and opportunities for informal contacts with parents 'in order to encourage their confidence and their understanding of the nursery school' must be seen, against this background, as bold and imaginative.

There is no doubt that a school takes risks in pursuing such a systematic policy of parental involvement. From the observations made, and from numerous contacts with parents themselves, it was possible to conclude that the 'open-door' policy was generally appreciated and has the effect of reducing tension. A small minority of disturbed people occasionally created difficulties, but seemed to be skilfully managed and supported. The milieu created for the children reflected the belief that involving parents – enhancing their status as educators, paying attention to their needs as well as to the children's – will produce improvements in the children's school record at a later age. There are a priori grounds for this hypothesis, particularly in the US Head Start evaluation already discussed.

An evolutionary model of collaborative learning

There are various ways in which neighbourhood centres can develop. Several of them have been tried in Hull and elsewhere, with different degrees of success. Perhaps the most common procedure has been for a council, often responding to some crisis in community relations, to provide money for a building. This is sometimes rejected by those for whom it was intended on the grounds that they were not consulted, which has happened in Manchester, Liverpool and Bristol. Neighbourhood centres have often enjoyed initial success that has tended to fade in the course of time, because the main impetus has come from outside or from a pressure group whose interests are satisfied with the attainment of premises.

The North Hull Neighbourhood Centre was more strongly based because it grew slowly, in response to statements of need by parents at McMillan Nursery and by other adults in the local community. This evolutionary process enabled achievements at each stage to be consolidated, and appeared more likely to achieve lasting results than provision based on the autocratic, paternalistic or response-to-pressure-group models.

A condition of the evolutionary model's success is that new members should continually be introduced so that the work-load is distributed and as many people as possible have the opportunity to gain experience. Despite the expressed doubts of some members of the committee, it was clear that this process had been occurring over the years, though perhaps on a more limited scale than might have been hoped. A critical point did seem to have been reached; this was recognised by those involved, and the extending of active committee membership was pursued by every means available. Inter-disciplinary co-operation between various branches of the 'caring' professions was a key feature of the Neighbourhood Centre's work. Clinics organised by health visitors have great potential for parent education, as has been amply demonstrated in other projects.[10]

There is scope for more use of child development materials, such as the Open University courses, used with great success by the project organised by the Community Education Development Centre in Salford and Leicestershire. 'Family matters' groups were led by a qualified teacher, who was also a single parent with four young children. The impact of this group on the women was observable in terms of both the products (written work, statistical summaries of a neighbourhood survey, drama and singing) and increased self-confidence and self-esteem – strongly manifested in the group's entertainments at an open evening I attended. Interesting activities, based on neighbourhood needs, were flourishing. Impressive artwork was on display. The pensioners' club and the parent-and-toddler club both organised by volunteers, were attracting viable groups.

The range and style of the Neighbourhood Centre's activities can be seen from the following timetable.

Mondays	*Parents' Committee Meeting* First Monday of each month	*Pensioners' Club* Bingo, singing, tea and biscuits. Contact: Maureen.	*Women's Keep-Fit* Dance-exercise to music. Contact: Rose.

Tuesdays	*Parent–Toddler Club* 9.30 a.m. 18 mths to 3 yrs. Contact: Gill.	*Community Health Clinic* Starting 16 October. Health Visitors in attendance. Attractive play area for children.	*Men's Gym Club* Weight-lifting and keep-fit. Contact: John.
Wednesdays	*Parent–Toddler Club* 9.30 a.m. 18 mths to 3 yrs. Contact: Gill.	*McMillan/ Fifth Avenue Workshop* Contact: Mrs Rice.	*Women's Keep-Fit* Dance exercise.
Thursdays	*Sue's Club* Sewing/craft activities, 9.30 a.m. Crèche available. Contact: Sue.	*Adult Education Class* Contact group. Crèche available. Contact: Kath.	*Men's Gym Club* Contact John.
Fridays	*Adult Education Class* Painting and drawing class, 9.30–11.45.	*Adult Education Class* Yoga. Relaxation for ladies with popular leader.	

In particular, the Neighbourhood Centre was successful in identifying new community leaders. Women who have not previously been involved in any kind of public work have taken active roles as chairperson, treasurer and secretary and have demonstrated clearly that they are capable of accepting the responsibility of raising funds and administering them. A necessary condition of the evolutionary model's success is that the official leader should be willing to hand over responsibility to the parent volunteers. There are few examples in British education of this process being carried to completion. The withdrawal of the Neighbourhood Centre leader to the status of co-opted committee member was, in the circumstances, a courageous and significant step. The indications were that those volunteer parents called on to accept officer-level responsibilities were responding competently and enthusiastically.

Conclusions

The various initiatives undertaken under the title the Neighbour-hood Centres Project constituted coherent, well-documented and replicable educational experiments and could be considered very good value for the modest funds invested. The McMillan Nursery School extended the normal programme for involving the parents of young children (1) within the school premises and (2) through community development in separate premises. The foundations of a neighbourhood family service were laid. The North Hull Neighbourhood Centre demonstrated that an evolutionary model of community development has the potential to produce a viable, self-sustaining organisation, and to identify new community leaders. Although its achievements were unusual, there are many other centres with similar objectives; the following brief account of one will support this assertion.

Pen Green Centre, Corby

It seems somehow easier to arrange the sharing of 'complementary expertise' between professionals and the parents of *young* children. At Pen Green Centre in Northamptonshire the objective is to provide 'a comprehensive service for parents and their young children in a friendly and stimulating environment'.[11] At a conference where this work was described, the session was enlivened by a contribution from one of the parents. This was enormously popular among the delegates, as living proof that the community really existed and could be reached.

Clearly, something was stirring in Corby. The Pen Centre was providing nursery education on a sessional basis from 9 a.m. to 9 p.m. each day, and a range of activities and facilities for parents that included: support group for children with special needs; toy library; training course for 'family friends' volunteers; drop-in coffee, friendship and play-group; baby group for parents and 0–1 age group; aerobics for parents and staff; welfare rights training course for single parents; yoga for parents; health workshop; workshop alternative health care (acupuncture, homoeopathy, etc.), plus 'men's issues'; free pregnancy-testing service run by volunteers;

Open University course for parents; single parents' group, self-support and crèche; moot group discussion on issues, e.g. glue-sniffing, drug abuse.

The Pen Green Centre cannot be far from achieving its objective in terms of the quantity and quality (confirmed by the parent representative) of its activities. A particularly interesting offshoot was a 'whole health shop'. About twenty people regularly attended these collaborative health education sessions; some of them were referrals from health visitors or social services, but most came for the company and interest. Sessions have included: after a baby and breast-feeding; depression and anxiety; family counselling; head infestation and skin disorder; developmental assessment; first steps towards a healthy diet; dealing with your GP; food allergies; pre-conceptual care; care during pregnancy; at the birth; child sex abuse; grief and loss; childhood ailments; make a medicine chest; the role of a social worker; feelings, after a baby; teenagers; contraception; stress; miscarriage and still birth; anorexia; menopause; coping on a low income; cervical cancer; infantile sexuality; pre-menstrual tension; psychiatric illness in the community; care of feet; sudden infant death; hearing difficulties; fostering and adoption; water safety; the politics of alternative health.

Although there were restraints on the further development of the Pen Green services – sixty-eight children having to be cared for and educated – three particular ambitions were being pursued. It was hoped to open parent centres in three nearby schools, to expand the use of the toy library and bookshop by making them into mobile services and to regularise relationships with the local community centre. The latter process was being aided by the growing use of Pen Green by outside agencies such as child and family guidance workers, health visitors and educational psychologists. The form of usage would seem to have been beneficial to all concerned:

> Many of the core group of professionals from other agencies who have worked with parent groups at the centre for nearly two years have said that this experience has changed their practice. Parents evaluate the work of the professsional, and feedback is always given. We feel that there is a much more flexible, informal approach, and the style adopted by many of our colleagues is far less didactic.[12]

PART THREE

Ways Forward

Only a few stubborn ones still blunder on, painfully, out of the luxuriant world of their pretensions into the desert of mortification and reward.

Patrick White, *Voss*

Our civilisation is founded on greed and fear but in the lives of common men the greed and fear are mysteriously transmuted into something nobler.

George Orwell, *Keep the Aspidistra Flying*

Figure 11.1   Why I Dislike School
by M. Etienne

There are many reasons why I dislike school, but they all culminate in one phrase, 'the system'. Our system is the same as the African slaves of many years ago, only it is concealed behind a mask of time. This mask provides it with an air of respectability. From the time you are born you can be counted as one of the many inside the fences which contain the human race and determine what you are allowed to do, and how and when you are allowed to do it.

School is only the beginning of a cycle which succeeds in totally wasting a person's time and and consequently their life. Any deviation from this route politically or otherwise is frowned upon.

It is not possible to live apart from society, as rules and laws will not allow for individuality to such an extent. The system could not survive if people started striking out for themselves and so the people at the top of the hierarchy would not retain their position which allows them to do as they please and keep others in their control.

One of the many problems with school is that it is not free enough in its attitude. For instance, any literature with political emphasis is not allowed to be printed in publications inside school. In my opinion any good piece of writing should be allowed to go to as wide an audience as possible because apart from enjoyment it can also stimulate people's minds about certain subjects. Rules like this do more harm than good.

Petty school rules and traditions only serve to provide animosity from pupils towards their teachers and these are only the tip of the iceberg.

The whole concept of school is wrong. There is something basically false about the standards set and positions held in school. I feel that a teacher is an equal and therefore does not have the right to expect standards from me which I cannot expect from him or her, i.e. if I open a door and hold it open for a teacher I expect the teacher to say 'thank you', as I would do.

If I could I would like to escape the whole system of life completely because of its hypocrisy and unfairness.[1]

CHAPTER 11

What professionals might do about themselves

It may be that my experience has given me a distorted view. I have spent much time among teachers who are enthusiastic about their jobs, imaginative in their approaches and apparently skilful and kindly in their handling of 'difficult' youngsters. At conferences all these qualities are in evidence, although some self-critical people have been heard to wonder aloud whether this is anything more than 'professional bellowing to professional across the primeval swamp'.

A considerable range of good practice has been surveyed in Chapters 6 to 10. I look at this immense effort and (with the help of Middleton and Weitzman)[2] set it in the context of the history of state education from the end of the eighteenth century. I read Middleton's dedication 'to the several generations of civic leaders who at council, committee, board and other meetings have spent countless unpaid hours in consultation and argument to further the provision of school and college places for everyone'.[3] To all this one can now add countless well-paid hours provided by personnel from the Manpower Services Commission. I read the words of the then Secretary of State for Social Services who wrote in 1974, no doubt in all sincerity:

> I have long been concerned that crippling social, material and emotional deprivations and miseries continue to be passed from generation to generation. This problem has remained despite the continuing development of our health, education and social services and the devoted work of those who provide them.[4]

The best minds of the (then) Social Science Research Council were called to bear upon the thesis of the cycle of deprivation (they found that there wasn't one). Mia Kellmer Pringle was commissioned to write *The Needs of Children*, where she stated 'ten child-care commandments'[5] These were presumably accepted by Sir Keith Joseph, for he called it a 'compelling and fascinating book' and 'a valuable basis for further thinking about development of our strategies for family support'.[6] The first of these commandments was: 'Give continuous, consistent, loving care.' Yet the school system has, and especially since Sir Keith Joseph became Secretary for Education, steadily declined in its capacity to provide this kind of support. It is appalling to contemplate the extent to which courageous policy-making has produced almost the diametric opposite to its publicly stated intentions.

I look at the conclusion to the piece by the secondary-school pupil in London – Figure 11.1 – and wish that the system did not present itself in such bleak terms. The troubles compound as the child enters secondary school, but the proper time to influence a child's *attitudes* to education is, ideally, before he or she is born (as we may have seen happening in Coventry); certainly in the earliest years of his or her life and school years. This book has suggested that much greater emphasis should be placed on social situations, motivation and support in the family and community. The case has been argued for educating with parents, and some achievements of parents and professionals have been recorded, when they have been working in reasonable harmony. The next stages concern parents' self-education and community involvement, so that those who have themselves gained so little from the education system might acquire more positive attitudes to communicate to their children. The cycle of *failure* is real enough, but it has been shown that it can be broken.

To facilitate this process, however, requires considerable changes in the attitudes and performance of teachers. The case study in Chapter 4 has shown how painfully and reluctantly some will undertake it. What must be done? First, there is a need to root out the patronising attitudes and occasional racism that sometimes determine the outcomes of negotiations between teachers (and lecturers), parents and pupils. Second, more flexible learning systems need to be developed, taking advantage of new learning theories and methods of presentation. Third, the time is long overdue for a more sophisticated analysis of the term 'parents', since parents vary

considerably in their attitudes towards their children's formal education. Fourth, the notion of 'professionalism' has to be subjected to
serious examination, to take account of changing conditions; here
again, we should not ignore the vigorous efforts of teachers and
social workers to evolve common working and training systems.

Changes in attitude

Some of the best contributions in the Swann Report are contained in
appendices. This is certainly true of the second chapter on 'the factors
contributing to underachievement', where a masterly paper by
Macintosh and Mascie-Taylor illuminates a rather laboured refuta-
tion of the claim that IQ scores can be interpreted to show genetic
differences between ethnic groups.[7] I have never been able to understand why this question is of any interest to educationists. The job of
the teacher is to assist the child to grapple with his/her learning
difficulties, and to rise to his/her maximum potential. The only purpose of a measure of intelligence, for the teacher, should be to illumi-
nate the learning strengths and to indicate the learning weaknesses of
a particular learner.

There are much better ways of measuring potential and much
wider interpretations of intelligence than the antique IQ test.
Macintosh accurately interprets the motives that have inflated the
importance of IQ scores:

> the possibility that there might be significant and ineradicable differ-
> ences in the average IQ of different social, ethnic or racial groups has
> been thought by some to justify prejudice or discrimination against all
> member of the groups with lower scores.[8]

But the distinction is spurious because of the large differences *within*
groups. We do not in any case discriminate against all groups with
lower-than-average IQ scores:

> No one has ever suggested that we should discriminate against twins;
> but there is excellent evidence that the average IQ of twins is about
> five points below that of the rest of the population. We do not think
> that this matters, and we should rightly question the good sense or
> good will of anyone who claimed that it did.[9]

Those who are eager to go on with these IQ arguments are doing
great harm. No British central or local government has ever accepted

such arguments, and has certainly not acted upon them. There are very much more useful things for teachers to be doing than dredging up Jensen and Eysenck, even if only to refute them. This particular spectre will not go away, however; it is too deeply rooted in certain psyches. It *has* to be refuted regularly.

The attitudes of home–school liaison teachers in Blackburn can be cited as polar opposites to these negative and destructive fixations. Several went to great lengths to inform themselves and their colleagues about the local Muslim community. An excellent example of such work was a booklet entitled *A Way of Life: The Muslim Community in Hyndburn and Rossendale* by Jackie Smallridge, published by the local Community Relations Council.[10] In her introduction, she acknowledged the assistance she received from all sections of the community; she firmly believed that the process of compiling such a document was useful in itself, as a means of bringing people together. Many of these teachers were learning community languages, in an attempt to widen and deepen their understanding of the culture of the minority group they wished to serve. Their starting position is a positive one: that the children, although probably speaking little or inaccurate English, are the products of an old, rich and complex culture, and speak a mother tongue that has the same attributes as English and can be drawn upon in providing an appropriate educational milieu.

Such a milieu, whatever kind of disadvantage it is hoping to reduce, will share these positive and undogmatic attitudes towards human potential. Howard Gardner has argued that all human beings are born with the potential to develop a multiplicity of intelligences, most of which are overlooked by the test batteries that yield the IQ score upon which so much tends to be based; the potential for musical accomplishment, for example, has been universally esteemed throughout human history, but it finds no place in an IQ test:

> The skilled use of one's body has been important in the history of the species for thousands, if not millions, of years . . . [but] a description of the use of the body as a form of intelligence may at first jar. There has been a radical disjunction in our recent cultural tradition between the activities of reasoning, on the one hand, and the activities of the manifestly physical part of our nature . . . this divorce between the 'mental' and the 'physical' has not infrequently been coupled with a notion that what we do with our bodies is somehow less privileged,

less special, than those problem-solving routines carried out chiefly through the use of language, logic or some other relatively abstract symbolic system.[11]

New approaches to learning and presentation

Schools are supposed to offer a broad curriculum suitable for the development of different intelligences. Not many succeed in achieving the right level of flexibility, and even when they make strenuous efforts to do so, few obtain parental support.[12] Such an approach is largely negated by the present trend towards a curriculum based upon teacher-determined objectives, orientated towards a world of work (no matter that the jobs do not exist, nor that when they are created they may require different skills from those being learned). Some colleges of further education possess the capacity and the will to respond to this new situation, and offer menu-driven courses that feature wide student choices. Their courses are administered within an adult education format, where students are encouraged and expected to take some role in negotiating their own curriculum.

Even within this friendly and flexible system, teachers often find it difficult to overcome the belief, in the words of the Pink Floyd's pop song, that 'We don't need no education.' Students fail to register, and many who do soon drop out. Many more could be attracted and retained, according to Thomas and Harri-Augstein, if teachers and others paid more attention to self-organised learning:

> Many people leave school (or further education) believing that effective learning consists of receiving established systems of objective knowledge in well-organised pre-digested forms. Such impersonal knowledge is either rejected or it remains separated from real-life experience and can only be used for limited predetermined purposes in limited predetermined situations. Such people may have learned how to be taught but they have not learned how to learn.[13]

The Pink Floyd may have been making better points than was immediately apparent. They were demonstrably achieving one of the currently applauded goals of the education system – they were self-employed. They were also demonstrating considerable competence in several skills regularly featured in MSC lists: they had acquired a good self-image; they had developed a capacity to work both individually and as members of a team; they had mastered musical instruments to a usable professional level; they had achieved market-place success. Many of these achievements were fostered by their 'education' – by which they meant 'schooling' – but their song does not express gratitude for the opportunities that had been provided. Schools urgently need to consider ways and means of shedding their image as being inimical to styles and contents of learning other than the 'academic' or the purely functional (i.e. training youngsters to be 'followers' as opposed to 'leaders').

I remain optimistic and curious about the effects of the vast expansion of the means for self-instruction available through computers, linked to other media such as audio and video cassettes. These systems are, in themselves, classless, but the knowledge of how to use them is already passing into middle-class hands and could still further widen the gap between the disadvantaged groups and others in the community. A hopeful sign, however, has been the ready acquisition of high technology by pop groups and the easy familiarity displayed by young people in their use of computers as games machines.

Reconsidering 'parents'

Sophisticated programmes must also take account of the various stances adopted by parents. Five different stances have been identified:[14]

(1) 'Work ethic' parents, who see school as a means of getting a good job, emphasise standards, formality and examinations. They view the current breakdown of discipline in schools as due to a widespread neglect of the basics.

(2) 'Distance' parents, who express a desire *not* to become involved with teachers, although not necessarily because they are not interested. They prefer to use other sources of information to find out about the school and to judge their children's progress.

(3) 'Familiar' parents, who give the impression that they have the relevant background knowledge. They usually adopt a supportive stance *vis-à-vis* the school.

(4) Parents who prefer to use their own 'observations', since they are sceptical about information gleaned directly from the teacher.

(5) Parents who 'defer' to the teacher's judgements.

Schools need to take account of these different attitudes and responses. For example, 'distance' parents require an 'equal partners' approach to maintain their dignity, whereas 'deference' parents need an authoritative statement from the school before they become involved. More formal approaches may be appropriate and sufficient for some parents but not for others. Home–school consultations, then, have to be conducted in different ways according to the stances adopted by parents.

A new professionalism

Meeting the educational needs of disadvantaged pupils requires changes in the traditional roles performed by teachers, social workers, health visitors and others. This possibility has been canvassed regularly over the last fifteen years,[15] and some of the boundary problems were brought out in Chapter 4. In the widely read *Children in Distress*, Alec Clegg argued:

> To deal with these problems a teacher–social worker is required – preferably a man or woman trained both as a teacher and as a caseworker
> . . . he [*sic*] should be the link man between the schools and the social services department, the police, the medical authorities, the probation officers and all likely to be acquainted with domestic distress and the need for help.[16]

A strong movement is at present developing in Britain around the theme 'family education'. Those who work under this banner take little interest in traditional boundaries, preferring to contribute expertise when, and in the manner, it is requested. This point-of-view was strongly advocated at a conference organised by the Community Education Development Centre in 1985. In a useful contribution, Welling suggested that the emphasis should be on habilitation rather than rehabilitation, on self-determined change rather than on the cure for some supposed disease: 'The traditionally authoritarian, role-frustrating, isolating approach of the professional has largely failed and other options which put the prime role of parents as educators should be contemplated.'[17] Mary Warnock, however, provided a spirited defence of 'professionalism', although fully accepting that parents must be involved:

> A professional teacher, like a professional general practitioner, must have as part of his professional expertise (and I think this goes equally for social workers and others who work with families) the ability to make the best of, and use, the non-professionals. In the teachers' case this means the ability to bring parents into education whenever it can help the child to do so and to keep parents out when it is best for the child, but with tact and understanding.[18]

This prescription was demonstrated in action at the special school studied in Chapter 9.

Whatever else, the role defined by the term 'professional' should include a capacity for systematic change. Being a professional does not require a rigid adherence to a predetermined role. Indeed, one of the hallmarks of the successful professions has been just this capacity to adapt and redefine their own expertise, together with the ability to convince others that their expertise is still genuine, useful and relevant.

There has been little informed discussion about the inter-professional disputes that are likely to ensue as teachers and others increasingly refuse to be constrained by traditional boundaries. Yet, as the case study of Downton Park School in Chapter 4 showed only too well, such disputes can seriously hamper progress. Teachers especially deserve the courtesy of clear guidelines, so that they know where to look for their professional justification. Providing such guidance, negotiating the terms within and between the professions – this is the way to ensure that teachers co-operate in changing the definition of their role *vis-à-vis* parents. The teachers would in my view be wise to lay emphasis upon their expertise as managers of learning and arrangers of learning opportunities, while simultaneously making strenuous efforts to upgrade these skills by keeping in touch with the huge changes being wrought through high technology. The primacy of the school as the locus of learning has already been challenged; the wise course is to accept and welcome these new sources of learning, to shift the emphasis to the process rather than the product. According to Thomas and Harri-Augstein, there exists the possibility of developing a language for negotiating changes in learning capacity that enables individuals 'to take control of the ways they learn from experience. . . . In the crisis-ridden conditions which prevail in much of contemporary society, where the "valued learning products" of today can easily become the chains restricting tomorrow's growth',[19] the managing of these new ways of thinking about learning becomes a crucial task. This is an exacting and potentially very rewarding job, but the tools to carry it out remain to be forged. Figure 11.2 indicates some of the implications for teacher training.

Figure 11.2   The new professionalism: implications for training

Post-experience level
Issues for negotiation and resolution
  (1) A redefinition of the role of the professional teacher to incorporate the knowledge, skills and expertise of parents.
  (2) Shifting the burden of the compensatory model.
  (3) Identifying determinants of change within a school.
  (4) Pursuing problems and policies, overcoming administrative obstacles, motivating staff, mobilising resources.

Knowledge
  (5) Minority group cultures; languages?
  (6) Learning theory, especially the management of self-organised learning in home and school environments.
  (7) Of other disciplines and agencies.

Skills
  (8) Dealing with other teaching staff, parents, wide range of professional and voluntary workers.
  (9) Record-keeping, evaluation.

Initial level
  (10) Resisting compensatory stereotypes.
  (11) Knowledge of minority cultures.
  (12) Learning theory, especially related to language and reading development.
  (13) Experience of self-organised learning.

Implication: at both levels, experiential learning is the only way to ensure that academic learning becomes *action* learning.

Especially at the post-experience level, training should become very precise, geared to the specific requirements of the job as defined, with opportunities to develop and practice the new skills under supervision. Each school should contrive to produce a statement of its training needs, so that the providing training establishment can negotiate a course content with the school and the nominated 'trainee'. This would be a vast improvement on the present hit-and-miss system of seconding teachers for full-time in-service training of a general kind (although the specific requirements can certainly be met within a more general framework if the second-ing school is prepared to take the trouble to state its needs). What I am urging is the same kind of devolution of responsibility, the same acceptance of self-organised learning, as we have already identified as a pre-requisite between school and parents. There is nothing airy-fairy about this scheme. since examples of such devolution have been given in Chapter 9 and elsewhere throughout the book. Good examples unfortunately do not make a good system; but they pro-vide the basis for a training programme and markers to reassure others who are trekking over the rough, upland terrain, in thick mist.

CHAPTER 12

What professionals might do with parents

This book has referred to a number of experiments that have improved the educational opportunities of children, in the short and long run, through various forms of collaborative learning. It is my hope that they provide some guide for a more productive use of the school system. Taken together, these observations suggest that a positive answer can be given to questions posed by Finch: 'Can the recipients of education successfully resist its controlling features? Can they turn the situation to their own advantage?'[1] There are comparatively few examples of parents being able to grasp the possibilities, but in Coventry, Liverpool, Manchester, Hull and Bradford enough has been witnessed to convince most people that communities *can* operate in and around the education system to produce noteworthy improvements. Many dedicated professionals are working effectively, acquiring new skills and even learning community languages. Despite the bad press that schools usually receive, many parents express great satisfaction and occasionally fight to preserve a school that they feel is serving their children well.

The small-scale experiment in parental collaboration reported in Chapter 10 demonstrates that devolution of responsibility can be achieved within the education system. The outcomes were entirely beneficial, as regards the effects on parents, on the school, on the children and on the community as a whole. No threats occurred to the smooth operation of the nursery school and the community centre.

It is a proper course of action for those who are disadvantaged in a democratic society to become aware of the possibilities for action *within* the system, to ensure that their children obtain the maximum benefit from what is provided or to campaign for the system to be adapted so that these benefits can be obtained. To be effective in this purpose requires certain skills. The raising of consciousness that precedes entry into the learning process is an important function of a community-based education system. The participatory model envisages parents active not only in supporting the school, but in supporting their children's learning. Parents are viewed as people exercising responsibility for their own lives, with more than marginal responsibility for the development and education of their offspring. This is perhaps nearer to high ideals than to any instrumental definition of education; but it can be defended at the lowest level on the grounds that an interest in dialogue and reasoning is preferable to an interest in violence and petrol bombs. The professional educator really has no choice but to keep on keeping on in this faith.

Continuity and partnership

Some relatively neglected Oxford University research concluded that no form of early learning will in itself benefit a child academically unless the impetus is maintained through his/her school years.[2] It was established that several forms of pre-schooling gave children a head start, but these positive gains were often frittered away. Parents visited at home developed positive and lasting interest in their children's education, but little use was made of it by the schools.

With these facts in mind, the Hulme Van Leer Project in Manchester had among its objectives the 'longer involvement of parents in the education system'.[3] The Hulme Project was organised by two qualified teachers and two trained nursery nurses, and was established in one of the flats in a gigantic deck-access block. Good home–school relationships were developed by linking the project with the schools, and by providing a neutral meeting-place for parents and teachers. Project staff worked with the schools to promote parental involvement and to encourage parents to become more interested in and aware of their children's education. Parents were encouraged to play with their children and to read to them in the project flat; books and toys were provided for home loan as well. The staff discussed all aspects of the education system with the parents, and many of the events and activities arranged from the flat provided specific opportunities for parents to gain a knowledge and understanding of how the education system works. The project provided information, in the form of leaflets and posters displayed in the flat, on adult education courses in the area. The staff would often bring these to the attention of the parents and encourage them to take advantage of the many facilities the Hulme area offered.

Similar work has been undertaken in Glasgow. 'Partnership in Education' is an action-research project located in Priesthill, a large council housing estate on the edge of the city. It is concerned with the education of children up the age of eight, but it does not take direct action with the children. Instead, the project's seven tutors work in partnership with the adults in the community who are most significant to children: parents, neighbours and local professionals. A number of research findings have been highlighted. It is assumed:

First, parents are the most significant adults in a child's education. Children are most likely to succeed at school and in society if:

- Parents enjoy taking time with their children.
- Families and neighbours talk and interact with children in ways that sharpen their minds.
- Children are encouraged at home and in the community to read and enjoy books.
- Home and school have a shared understanding of the school's task.

Secondly, the *power of words*: skill in putting ideas in order and in communicating them clearly is a powerful tool in school and in society. All project tutors are involved in raising parents' awareness of their own word power as well as of the importance of stimulating this power in their children.

Thirdly, concerning *group work*: partnership is helped to become real when the setting emphasises the essential equality of the human beings participating. Small groups are an easy way of sharing ideas and learning from each other. To allow participants to bring thought and action together the process used in all project programmes is one of reflected experience. Tutors try to work respectfully with parents, children and professionals in ways that allow shared experiences to be discussed. Plans for further steps are taken in the light of this reflection.

Women and children first?

Home Link in Liverpool was originally intended to be a traditional, early-childhood education programme, rather didactic, and with the emphasis on the child.[4] Over a period of years this evolved *under the guidance of the mothers themselves,* into a series of adult education courses covering topics related to welfare rights, women and health, women's studies, child development, and a drop-in facility and toy library. The shift was away from confident assertions about the form that effective early-childhood education might take and towards a community-based approach that convinced the women of the value of their own contribution to the mothering process – and also of their own value as individuals. Home Link rapidly became a project for women and children. In the early formulations there was still an assumption that men would become involved at some point. But the project workers came to accept the paramount needs of women, upon whom 'many and varied forces were together an increasing pressure, especially on mothers, making them at once more isolated and more responsible for children whose nurture they were less and less able to control'.[5] So it was women and children first. The institutions of the Welfare State, which are intended to provide support and guidance, seemed ironically rather to reinforce the initial sense of failure felt by these mothers, 'whose oppression is agonisingly apparent on such [council] estates'.[6] The project workers felt that to make progress it would be necessary to transfer power from 'professionals and bureaucrats' to local people. Increasingly, however, the Home Link workers came to share the sense of powerlessness felt by their clients: 'An awareness of the faults of a system does not necessarily lead to change. The individual feels powerless against the weight of the institution and the traditional systems'.[7] It is what A. H. Halsey called 'the classic dilemma of participatory democracy'.[8]

Various lessons can be drawn from Home Link's observation that small projects cannot hope to change deeply-rooted attitudes other than marginally. ('It is almost a cruel joke to expect small projects like Home Link to be anything but unsuccessful.')[9]

Lesson one was that very fundamental changes *have* been pioneered in this way. The Home Link workers, in more cheerful mood, noted the climate of opinion in British education changing, so that an increasing number of British schools were prepared to embrace some form of community education.

Lesson two was that projects should set themselves realistic objectives, the accomplishment of which is within the physical and financial capabilities of the personnel available. If a policy is adopted of encouraging people to state their needs, it is necessary to develop strategies for guiding them towards effective action – maybe even by involving those professionals who are paid to do this job! The skills acquired by project workers should surely include marshalling human resources. Not all professionals have the critical attitudes towards and dire influences on mothers that were recorded by Home Link in Liverpool; and even here Home Link worked with a health worker for one year, and there were some happy outcomes such as the organisation of a communal meal.

Palfreeman gave an account of groups organised by health visitors in similar, very difficult circumstances; it was significant that the title was 'Valuing Mothers'.[10] These groups, after initial problems, were organised by the mothers themselves in their own homes. They focused on aspects of child development, and some followed courses provided by the Open University. There would seem to be clear grounds for mutual contributions by professionals and para-professionals, but new styles of training and self-preparation are likely to be necessary, both before and during projects.

A school and family concordat?

Excellent though the foregoing work is, the focus of action in breaching the cycle of failure should probably be *within* the compulsory school system. This diversion of effort outside the school suits the entrenched professionals who dislike parent involvement in the schools and who rejected the Taylor Report (1977) as a 'busybody's charter'.[11] There has since been a shift in outward behaviour, if not in genuine belief, and an observable increase in the activity of parent governors. I have met many on my travels who vigorously and constructively represent a body of parental opinion previously unheard. Asian groups in Bradford have made full use of this platform to pursue their case against a headteacher whose published opinions made him a controversial figure.[12] The time might now be opportune to look closely at the substantial report from the EEC entitled *The Child Between* and particularly at its proposal for a 'concordat'.[13]

The report considers stages by which the school may change from being a self-contained organisation, with emphasis upon teacher autonomy and few contacts with parents, to a kind of school through which parents and teachers work as educational partners. It points out that it is easier for both parents and teachers *not* to act as partners. It suggests that focus should change from parental rights to parental obligations. At the heart of the concordat idea would be a *contract* between parents and the school. This could be a written understanding signed annually by parents, in return for which the state provides schooling to assist them in fulfilling their educational obligations established in the law.

Parents would sign that they *understand*

(1) that the prime responsibility for their child's education rests with them as parent(s);
(2) that their active support of the child's schooling will increase his/her likelihood of gaining maximum benefit from it.

Besides the expressions of understanding, parents would also agree to certain basic *actions*:

(3) to attend periodic private consultations about their child's progress;
(4) to read written reports sent by the school;
(5) to attend class meetings arranged by the school in regard to their child's class;
(6) to provide appropriate facilities, conditions and encouragement for homework when it is included in the syllabus;
(7) to support and assist the school's efforts to the best of their ability;
(8) to support the school's rules and arrangements, and to use their influence to ensure that their child does so too;
(9) to undertake to provide whatever information about the child is necessary for his/her educational advance;
(10) to undertake to abide by the decisions of their school's council and management.

The accounts in this book of parents from disadvantaged areas all over Britain have shown that they are for the most part serious and competent people who would respond well to this kind of clear and reasonable approach. Indeed, they do respond well to involvement in reading and other schemes, and such parental involvement has had considerable and widespread success. The main difficulty is perhaps that the suggested terms of this EEC concordat are so entirely in favour of the school. It looks like the communications model writ large, dressed in new authority. My hope would be that these terms are negotiable, as is suggested in the statement with which the EEC report concludes:

> Emphasis in this section has been upon duties, rather than upon rights; the duties of parents and teachers on behalf of the child. If we are to speak of rights, those of the child must be central. Access to schooling is only one step towards that elusive goal, equality of educational opportunity for the child. Perhaps just as important are:
>
> (1) Equality of active parental support for and involvement in schooling.
> (2) Equality of high professional commitment by teachers.[14]

Conclusion

The agonisingly slow movement of the maintained education system has been traced as it has begun to shift, through the efforts of central and local government, individual schools, teachers and projects funded by charitable trusts, away from a paternalistic and compensatory model and towards the outlines of a negotiated and participatory model. There is much to applaud. An abundance of strenuous activity has been undertaken. Genuine progress has been demonstrated in the delivery of services to pupils who enter the system under disadvantaged circumstances and who manifest special educational needs. The bad news is that the system treats some pupils much more favourably than others, distinguishing in favour of certain social classes, racial groups, geographical areas and types of ability or disability. A substantial proportion of the population feels that it is the victim of discrimination with, unfortunately, full justification.

Thus despite the well-intentioned work of many skilled and dedicated professionals over a long period, the education system moves towards the century's end in a state of confusion where injustice and waste are rampant. This is not inevitable. We have seen what excellent results can be expected when the users and providers of the education service agree on where they want it to go. The future belongs not to those who get the new technology – for it will quickly become universal – but to those societies that can organise themselves to use it effectively. The market-place, common sense and the general good demand an end to the waste caused by the unnecessary continuance of educational disadvantage.

Notes and References

1 Personal perspective

1. Lee, Laurie (1959), *Cider with Rosie*, Harmondsworth: Penguin.
2. Widlake, P. (1983), *How to Reach the Hard to Teach*, Milton Keynes: Open University Press.
3. Halsey, A. H. (1972), *Educational Priority: EPA Problems and Policies* (the Halsey Report), London: HMSO. Three other volumes have been published on the EPA Project: (1974) Vol. 2, *EPA Surveys and Statistics*; (1975) Vol. 3, *Curriculum Innovation in London EPAs*; (1975) Vol. 4, *The West Riding Project*; London: HMSO.
4. Widlake, P. (1981–3), *Evaluation Reports I–V*, Community Education Development Centre, Briton Road, Coventry CV2 4LF.
5. Widlake, P. (1982), *Unemployed Young Women in Coventry and Birkenhead*, Coventry: CEDC.
6. Central Advisory Council for Education (1967), *Children and their Primary Schools* (the Plowden Report), London: HMSO.
7. Middleton, N. and Weitzman, S. (1976), *A Place for Everyone: A History of State Education from the Eighteenth Century to the 1970s*, London: Gollancz.
8. Halsey (1972), op. cit.

2 Historical perspective

1. Halsey, A. H. (1981), *Change in British Society*, Oxford: Oxford University Press.
2. Committee of Higher Education (1963), *Higher Education* (the Robbins Report), London: HMSO.

3. Central Advisory Council for Education (1959), *Fifteen to Eighteen* (the Crowther Report), London: HMSO.

4. Central Advisory Council for Education (1963), *Half Our Future* (the Newsom Report), London: HMSO.

5. McVicker Hunt, J. (1969), *The Challenge of Incompetence and Poverty*, Chicago: University of Illinois Press.

6. Bloom, B. S. (1964), *Stability and Change in Human Characteristics*, New York: Wiley.

7. Westinghouse Learning Corporation (1969), *The Impact of Head Start: An Evaluation of the Effects of Head Start on Children's Cognitive and Affective Development*, Washington, DC.

8. Tizard, B. (1974), *Early Childhood Education*, Slough: NFER, p. 4.

9. Zigler, E. and Valentine, J. (1979), *Project Head Start: A Legacy of the War on Poverty*, New York: Free Press.

10. Blank, M. (1974), in Tizard (1974), op. cit.

11. Ibid., p. 94.

12. Lewis, O. (1968), *La Vida: A Puerto Rican Family in the Culture of Poverty*, London: Panther.

13. Bereiter, C. and Engelmann, S. (1966), *Teaching Disadvantaged Children in the Pre-School*, Englewood Cliffs, NJ: Prentice-Hall.

14. Bernstein, B. (1959), 'A Public Language: Some Sociological Implications of Linguistic Form', *British Journal of Sociology*, 10, pp. 311–26; (1961), 'Social Class and Linguistic Development', in A. H. Halsey, J. Floud and C. Anderson (eds.), *Education, Economy and Society*, New York: Free Press.

15. Wilkinson, A. (1971), *The Foundation of Language: Talking and Reading in Young Children*, Oxford University Press.

16. Rogers, R. (1980), *Crowther to Warnock*, London: Heinemann.

17. Jencks, C. *et al.* (1972) *Inequality: A Reassessment of the Effects of Family and Schooling in America*, New York: Basic Books.

18. Young, M. and McGeeney, P. (1968), *Learning Begins at Home*, London: Routledge and Kegan Paul.

19. Leicester City Council (1979), *Leicester Inner Area Programme 1980–83*.

20. Sharp, R. and Green, A. (1975), *Education and Social Control: A Study in Progressive Primary Education*, London: Routledge and Kegan Paul.

21. Committee of Enquiry into the Education of Children from Ethnic Minority Groups (1985), *Education for All* (the Swann report), London: HMSO, pp. 7–8.

22. Douglas, J. W. B. (1964), *The Home and the School*.

23. Sharp and Green (1975), op. cit.

24. Goode, J. (1982), '*The Development of Effective Home–School Programmes: A Study of Parental Perspectives on the Process of Reading*', unpublished M.Phil. thesis, University of Nottingham.

25. HM Inspectorate of Schools (1984), *Slow learning and less successful pupils in secondary schools. Evidence from some HMI visits*. London: DES.

3   The communications model: an inner-city multicultural primary school

1. Schonell, F. and Schonell, E., (1939, Revised 1971) *Happy Venture Reading Scheme* – continued through 8–11 years as *Wide Range* and *Reading On* series, London: Oliver and Boyd.
2. See also Widlake, P. 'Primary School Practice and Pupil Success', in M. Marland (ed.), *Education for the Inner City*, London: Heinemann.

4   The communications model: group work in a day special school

1. Widlake, P. (1980), *Evaluation Report*, unpublished, Manchester Polytechnic.
2. Hunt, S. (1974), *Parents of the ESN*, Manchester, Elfreda Rathbone Association.
3. Widlake (1980), op. cit.
4. Hunt (1974), op. cit.
5. Widlake (1980), op. cit
6. Hunt (1974), op. cit., pp. 8–9.
7. Widlake (1980), op. cit.

5   Joys and sorrows of home–school liaison work

1. Cleveland Project: funded under the Urban Aid Grants, which by 1977 had reached Phase 14 and were supporting a considerable number of projects involving teachers and social workers.
2. Project leader's report (1977).
3. Macleod, F. (1984), *Parents in Partnership: Involving Muslim Parents in their Children's Education*, Coventry: CEDC.
4. Silver, H. (1965), *The Concept of Popular Education: A Study of Ideas and Social Movements in the Early Nineteenth Century*, London: McGibbon & Kee. Silver used the term 'popular education' 'as an after-the-event shorthand to cover a range of thinking about the education of the poor and deprived, from the most limited and condescending charitable approach to the labouring classes, to the most ambitious plans for national education'. This attempt at a definition fits usefully into the present study, which deals with the situation 150 years later. It is worth taking a larger historical perspective than that already attempted, however, in order to see how much has been accomplished. The problem is now often the failure of those so defined to take up the educational opportunities provided.

6 Lessons to be learned from the communications model

1. HM Inspectorate of Schools (1985), *Better Schools*, London: DES, pp. 1–2.
2. Willis, P. (1985), *Research Report on Unemployed in Wolverhampton*, Wolverhampton: Social Services Department.
3. Mangham, I. (1979), *The Politics of Educational Change*, London: Associated Business Press.
4. Hunt, S. (1974), *Parents of the ESN*, Manchester: Elfreda Rathbone Association, p. 28.
5. Committee of Enquiry into the Education of Children from Ethnic Minority Groups (1985), *Education for All* (the Swann Report), London: HMSO.
6. Ibid. Annexe A.
7. Stone, M. (1981), *The Education of the Black Child in Britain: The Myth of Multiracial Education*, London: Fontana.
8. Swann Report (1985), op. cit., p. 198.
9. Aitken, R. (1985), paper at CEDC Family Education Conference, Coventry Polytechnic.
10. *Wolverhampton Express and Star,* 1985.
11. Lorenz, K. (1963), *On Aggression*, London: Methuen.
12. Ibid.
13. Eibl-Eibesfeldt, I. (1970), *Love and Hate*, London: Methuen.
14. Russell, Bertrand (1971), *Principles of Social Reconstruction*, Allen & Unwin.
15. Peters, R. S. (1976), in Dearden, R. F., Hirst, P. H. and Peters, R. S., *A Critique of Current Educational Aims*, London: Routledge & Kegan Paul.
16. Committee of Enquiry into the Education of Handicapped Children and Young People (1978), *Special Educational Needs* (the Warnock Report), London: DES.
17. Freire, P. (1973), *Pedagogy of the Oppressed*, Harmondsworth: Penguin.
18. Ibid., p. 19.
19. Ree, H. (1973), *Educator Extraordinary: A Biography of Henry Morris*, London: Longman.
20. Watts, J. (1977), *The Countesthorpe Experience*, London: Allen & Unwin; see also Fletcher, C., Caron, M. and Williams, W. (1985), *Schools on Trial*, Milton Keynes: Open University Press, chapter 3.
21. Fletcher, C. (1978), *The Challenges of Community Education Sutton-in-Ashfield, Nottinghamshire*, University of Nottingham; see also Fletcher, Caron and Williams (1985), op. cit.
22. Gillett, N. (1979), 'The Advantages of Community Schools', *New Era* 3, April-June 1979.
23. Midwinter, E. (1973), *Priority Education: An Account of the Liverpool Project*, Harmondsworth: Penguin. *Patterns of Community Education*, London: Ward Lock.

7 Collaborative learning: a whole–system approach

1. Firth, G. C. (1977), *Seventy-five Years of Service to Education: The Story of Coventry's Education Committee*, City of Coventry Education Committee. Documents on the work of the CEP have been published from time to time and are available from CEP, Southfields School, South Street, Coventry CV1 5EJ.
2. Widlake, P. and Macleod, F. (1984), *Raising Standards*, Coventry: CEDC.
3. A full account of the tests and research procedure is given in *Raising Standards*, op. cit. 'Reading for Meaning' is a multiple-choice cloze procedure test, i.e. instead of the deletions in a conventional cloze test there are four alternative words from which the child has to choose one. This 'eliminates the influence of writing ability on the reading results. In a conventional cloze test a child may know the right word that goes in a deletion, but may be unable to write it in an intelligible form; or he/she may be able to write the words, but the writing may be very time-consuming and tiring. The 'Reading for Meaning' test can thus be said to be a more 'pure' test of reading ability than a conventional cloze test'.
4. The criteria adopted in an analysis of schools undertaken by Coventry Education Department selected two main socio-economic indicators:
   (1) *Indicators of deprivation:* data for each school catchment area was selected from the 1981 Census relating to unemployment, possession of car, lone parents, housing. These variables do not of themselves necessarily indicate deprivation, but together they represent deprivation factors consistently identified in research by such bodies as the Child Poverty Action Group.
   (2) *Ethnic composition:* information was taken from two sources: (a) 1981 Census (but this does not reflect the ethnic origins of the population unless they are recent arrivals; (b) Coventry Education Department (details of ethnic background of school pupils). All the schools included in the Coventry sample scored high on some of these indicators. Surprisingly for a city that has figured so prominently in the motor-car industry, the city average for households with no car was 43 per cent at the 1981 Census; one of the sample schools reached 74 per cent. The tables provided in the manual to the Hunter-Grundin Literacy Profiles seem to accept the designation of Educational Priority Area by local authorities as their basis. There are many discrepancies, but most indices used for this purpose include most of these indicators.

8 Parents, language and reading development

1. Central Advisory Council for Education (1967), *Children and their Primary Schools* (the Plowden Report), London: HMSO.
This was the first major report on primary education since those of Sir Henry Hadow in 1931 and 1933, and in the years immediately

following the Education Act 1944, government interest had been heavily concentrated on secondary education. Yet English primary schools were often referred to as the envy of the Western educational world. The Committee under Lady Plowden was asked to consider primary education in all its aspects and the transfer to secondary education. Their Report included descriptions of current ideas on education and child development, in the setting of particular home and neighbourhood conditions. It launched two key concepts – the need for positive discrimination, administered through educational priority areas; and the importance of parental involvement in a child's education. The latter is what I have in mind when I refer to 'going with the grain of the Plowden Report', together with its emphasis on imaginative methods, on 'finding out' rather than 'being told', on seeking to meet individual needs, on encouraging creativity, on broadening the curriculum without losing sight of the older virtues of 'neatness, accuracy, care and perseverance'.

2. This Survey was carried out as part of the routine work at the Community Education Development Centre, and has been used to provide information to Affiliates but has not previously been reported in this form. It is interesting because the answers to the questions show a consistency which is, apparently, nationwide and more detailed than other reports currently available.

3. Raven, J., (1980), *Parents, Teachers and Children*, London: Hodder and Stoughton.

4. Tizard, B. and Hughes, M. (1984), *Young Children Learning*, London: Fontana.

5. Ibid., p. 267.

6. Ferreiro, E. and Teberosky, A. (1982) *Literacy before Schooling*, London: Heinemann.

7. Mackay, D., Thompson, B. and Schaub, P. (1970) *Breakthrough to Literacy*, London: Longman.
   This Manual, and the set of materials associated with it, has been a very influential contribution to the teaching of reading and can be found in many infants schools in England and Wales, though not often being used in the manner envisaged by the authors. *Breakthrough* emphasises that 'reading matter for children should, from the beginning, be linked to their own spoken language'. Unlike 'traditional schemes', *Breakthrough* 'integrates the production (writing) and the reception (reading) of written language', using a set of apparatus called the Sentence Maker for this purpose. The approach falls within those usually described as language-experience, and its implementation generates controversies as fierce as when it was first introduced. For example, there appears to have been a regression towards the dismal practice of 'marking progress in reading by reference to the page number in a series of books', which Mackay and his colleagues hoped they were replacing with 'an explicit and carefully graded description of the chief processes involved in learning to read and write'.

8. Bettelheim, B. and Zelan, K. (1982), *On Learning to Read The Child's Fascination with Meaning*, London: Thames and Hudson.

9. Widlake, P. (1986), *The Salford and Leicester Project*, Evaluation Report, Coventry: CEDC.
10. Ibid.
11. Wells, G. (1985), *Language Development in the Pre-School Years*, Cambridge: Cambridge University Press.
12. E.g. Wells (1985), op. cit.; Tizard and Hughes (1984), op. cit. Two publications from the Birmingham University *Educational Review*, 1985, are worth mentioning at some length. *Helping Communication in Early Education* is a collection of six Papers, mostly by writers who also participated in a research project, the subject of a second publication *Early Education of Children with Communication Problems: particularly those from ethnic minorities*, edited by Margaret Clark. Among unexpected insights revealed through the use of radio microphones was the following:

    'When listening to the tape recordings, it was difficult to distinguish which children were from ethnic minorities and equally, on transcription, the differences in language skills varied as much for indigenous children as it did for those of Asian or Afro-Caribbean origin'.

    Chapters 3, 4 and 10 of the research report surveyed the language skills of children entering the reception class at ages varying between four and five years. Language attainments at many different levels were recorded: '. . . in each of these schools there were some children . . . who had impressive abilities to understand and respond to questions of high levels of complexity and perceptual distance . . . even when assessed in English, there were children within each ethnic group who were able to respond appropriately . . . likewise there were children of each ethnic background with very limited understanding of anything beyond simple labelling questions.'

9 Through the suspicion barrier

1. Raven, J. (1980), *Parents, Teachers and Children*, London: Hodder and Stoughton.
2. Lodge, P. and Blackstone, T. (1983), *Educational Policy and Educational Inequality*, Oxford: Martin Robertson.
3. Widlake, P. (1986), *The Salford and Leicester Project*, Evaluation Report, Coventry: CEDC.
4. Bastiani, J. (1978), *Written Communication between Home and School*, University of Nottingham.
5. Fletcher, C. (1983), *The Challenges of Community Education*, University of Nottingham. See also Fletcher, C., Caron, M. and Williams, W. (1985) *Schools on Trial*, Milton Keynes: Open University Press.
6. Widlake, P. (1986), op. cit.

10 Collaborative learning: small is beautiful?

1. The development of this centre, from its origins in McMillan Nursery School, has been extensively recorded by the initiators and co-ordinators, Margaret Rice and Patrick Doyle. The main publications are:

   Parental Involvement Project, North Humberside: McMillan Nursery School (May, 1982). An account of six weeks' work undertaken as a result of financial support from Humberside LEA for innovatory projects.

   Working with Parents and Professionals, Professional Centre for Teachers, Humberside College of Higher Education (July, 1983). A full account of the origins of the Neighbourhood Centre and of attempts to disseminate good practice, especially in the North Bransholme area of Hull. Contains lengthy accounts by the headteachers and an education welfare officer.

   Aspects of partnership in the Early Years, Professional Centre, Humberside College of Higher Education (1983). Full report and evaluation of a course for teachers held at Humberside College, March 1983.

   Under-Fives Council Newsletter 6, Humberside County Council. Includes articles by heads of North Bransholme primary schools on parent–toddler clubs, toy libraries, etc.

   The Neighbourhood Centre Projects, Hull, January 1983 to July 1984, Professional Centre, Humberside College of Higher Education. A succinct account of development during this period, containing personal accounts from headteachers, group leaders, committee members and others.

   Education in an Urban Environment: McMillan Nursery School – a Review, and future Possibilities, March 1984 to October 1984, by Margaret Rice. Contains the first proposal for a 'parent education centre'; summarises curriculum developments at the Neighbourhood Centre and expenditure of grants.

   'The Neighbourhood Centre Project, Hull', by Margaret Rice and Patrick Doyle, article for the *Van Leer Newsletter* (December 1984).

   Neighbourhood Centres Project, Hull, North Humberside, a report by Paul Widlake, Coventry: CEDC (March 1985).
2. Kellmer Pringle, M. (1971), *The Needs of Children*, London: Hutchinson, p. 39.
3. Zigler, E. and Valentine, J. (1979), *Project Head Start: A Legacy of the War on Poverty*, New York: Free Press, p. 447.
4. Ibid., p. 468.
5. Bruner, J. (1980), *Under-Fives in Britain*, London: Grant McIntyre.
6. Tizard, B. (1974), *Early Childhood Education – a Review of Research*, Slough: NFER. (1981), *Involving Parents in Nursery and Infant Schools*, London: Grant McIntyre.
7. Tizard, B., Mortimore, J. and Burchell, S. (1981), *Involving Parents in Nursery and Infants Schools*. London: Grant McIntyre.

8. Smith, T. (1980), *Parents and Pre-School*, London: Grant McIntyre.
9. Cyster, R. *et al.* (1980), *Parental Involvement in Primary Schools*, Slough: NFER.
10. E.g. Palfreeman, S. (1982), 'Valuing Mothers', *Journal of Comm. Education* Vol. 1, No. 4, Dec 1982.
11. Charlwood, M. (1986), 'Pen Green Centre for Under-Fives and their Families', report by centre leader, CEDC Family Education Conference, Coventry Polytechnic.
12. Ibid.

11 What professionals might do about themselves

1. From Nkosi, L. (ed.) (1978), *South Kilburn Voices*, London Borough of Brent Social Services Committee.
2. Middleton, N. and Weitzman, S. (1976), *A Place for Everyone: A History of State Education from the Eighteenth Century to the 1970s*, London: Gollancz.
3. Ibid.
4. Sir Keith Joseph (1974) quoted in Middleton, N. & Weitzman, S. op. cit.
5. Kellmer Pringle, M. (1974), *The Needs of Children*, London: Hutchinson, p. 159. Rutter, M. & Madge, N. (1976), *Cycles of Disadvantage*, London: Heinemann.
6. Sir Keith Jospeh (1974). Foreword to Kellmer Pringle, M. op. cit.
7. Macintosh, N. J. and Mascie-Taylor, C. G. N. (1985), in the Swann Report, op. cit.
8. Ibid.
9. Ibid. p. 148.
10. Smallridge, J. (1981), *A Way of Life: The Muslim Community in Hyndburn and Rossendale*, Lancashire: Community Relations Council.
11. Gardner, H. (1984), *Frames of Mind. The Theory of Multiple Intelligences*, New York: Basic Books.
12. Fletcher, C. (1983), *The Challenges of Community Education*, University of Nottingham.
13. Thomas, L. and Harri-Augstein, S. (1985), *Self-Organised Learning Foundations for a Conversational Science for Psychology*, London: Routledge and Kegan Paul.
14. Goode, J. (1982), *The Development of Effective Home–School Programmes: A Study of Parental Perspectives on the Process of Reading*, unpublished M.Phil. thesis, University of Nottingham.
15. E.g. Clegg, A. and Megson, B. (1968), *Children in Distress*, Harmondsworth: Penguin; Johnson, D. and Ransom, E. (1980), *Parents' Perceptions of Secondary Schools, in* Craft, M. et. al. (ed.) *Linking Home and School*; Armstrong, G. and Brown, F. (1979) *Five Years On*, University of Oxford: Social Evaluation Unit, Department of Social and Administrative Studies; Pugh, G. (1986), paper at CEDC Family Education Conference, Coventry Polytechnic.

16. Clegg, A. and Megson, B, op. cit.
17. Family Education Conference Report (1986), Coventry: CEDC.
18. Ibid.
19. Thomas, L. and Harri–Augstein, S. (1985), op. cit., p. 337.

12   What professionals might do with parents

1. Finch, J. (1984), *Education as Social Policy*, London: Longman.
 2. Armstrong, G. and Brown, F. (1979), *Five Years On A Follow-Up Study of the Long-Term Effects on Parents and Children of an Early Learning Programme in the Home*, University of Oxford: Social Evaluation Unit, Department of Social and Administrative Studies.
 3. Widlake, P. and Crow, G. (1982), *The Van Leer Hulme Project*. Evaluation Report, Coventry CEDC.
 4. Filkin, E. (Ed.) (1984), *Women and Children First: Home Link – A Neighbourhood Education Project*, The Hague: Van Leer Foundation.
 5. Ibid.
 6. Ibid.
 7. Ibid.
 8. Halsey, A. H. (1984), Foreword to Filkin, E., op. cit.
 9. Filkin, E. op. cit., p. 83.
10. Palfreeman, S. (1984), 'Valuing Mothers', *J. Comm.Ed*, Vol. 1, No. 4.
11. Department of Education and Science (1977), *A New Partnership for our Schools* (the Taylor Report), London: HMSO.
12. Mr. R. Honeybone was the headteacher of a 'middle-school' (children aged approximately 9–13 years) in Bradford. The vast majority of the students were Asian. He published an article in a small circulation, Right-wing journal called the *Salisbury Review,* which was critical of certain aspects of multi-cultural education policies. This provoked an uproar among the Asian parents of his students. He received strong backing from the headteachers' Union and lengthy legal proceedings eventually permitted him to resume his post. The parents organised a boycott and picketed the school, attracting enormous media attention and so intensifying the pressure on Mr. Honeybone that he accepted early retirement (1985).
13. Macbeth, A. (1984), *The Child Between: A Report on School-Family Relations in the Countries of the European Community*, London: HMSO (for EEC).
14. Ibid.

Index

Abraham Moss 49
A-Level 66
action research 2
Action Sport 4
Afro-Caribbean 3, 16
anthropologists 11
authority 6
age 8
Armstrong, G. and Brown, F. 125
Asians 45, 94, 128
Assessment of Performance Unit 5

Bastiani, J. 82
Batley 4
behaviourist school 69
Bereiter, C. and Engelmann, S. 12
Bernstein, B. 12
Bettelheim, B. 69
'Better Schools' 40
Birkenhead 4, 16
Blackburn 4, 114
Bloom, B. 10
Blank, M. 11
Bradford 4, 124, 128
'Breakthrough to Literacy' 69
Bristol 13
brochures 83
Bruner, J. 105
Bullock report 73

Cambridgeshire 49
Centre on Educational Disadvantage 5
Clark, P. 82
Clegg, A. 120
Cleveland 33
codes, elaborated and restricted 12
community development officer 25

community education 6, 48–52, 117
Community Education Development
    Centre 4, 120
Community Education Project 55–8,
    59, 72
community leaders 108
Community Relations Commission 94
community school 2
concordat 128–130
conferences
    Family Education Unit, C.E.D.C.
    120–1
    Community Education Association 5
consciousness 28, 125
cooperation 6, 45–8
Corby 109
Countesthorpe 49
Coventry 6, 16, 45, 63, 64, 124
Crowther Report 9
Croydon, London Borough of 64
Culture
    'cultural deprivation' 6, 43
    of poverty 11–12
    Caribbean 3
Curriculum
    environment 57
    general 118
    home tutoring 57
    music 19
    lack of planning 40
cycle of deprivation 115
cycle of failure 115

Deficits 12, 14
Department of Education and Science
    Circular 11/67, 14

Derbyshire 64
dialogue 5
disadvantage 15, 41, 125, 129–130
    criteria of 136
disadvantaged pupils 2, 4
Douglas, J. W. B. 16
Doyle, P. 103
Drop-in groups 97–8
Dublin 5

education
    adult 1, 56
    compensatory 13, 37, 43
    early childhood 11, 56, 95–6, 105–6
    Education Act 1944 6
    educational opportunities 7, 119
    expectations 19, 22
    multicultural 24–5, 43
    philosophies of 43–4, 47, 125
    policies 6, 7, 44–5
    popular 1, 37
    special educational needs 8
    standards 59–62
Education Welfare Officer 89
Educational Priority Areas 2, 19
    E.P.A. Project 5, 13, 14
European Economic Community 50,
    128, 129
Eibl-Eibesfeldt, I. 47
Eliot, T. S. 5
enrichment 12
ethnic groups 8, 116
ethnography 3
ethnologists 47
evolutionary model 106–9
Experimental World Literacy Project *see*
    Literacy
Eysenck, H. J. 117

Fairbairn, A. 49
Ferreiro, E. and Teberosky, A. 69
Finch, J. 124
followers 119
Freire, P. 48
frames of mind 117

Gardner, H. 117
Gender 8
Gillett, N. 51
Glasgow 126
Goode, J. 16

group work 27–32, 126
    success of 31–2
Gujarati 94

Hackney, London Borough of 64
Halsey, A. H. 2, 7, 9, 127
    Halsey report 13
    see also Educational Priorities Areas
Handsworth 45
'hard to teach' 2
Harri-Augstein, S. 118, 121
Harvey, B. 50
Hazel Primary School and Community
    Centre 82
Head Start 10, 104–5
Health Visitors 107
Her Majesty's Inspectors of Schools 16,
    40
Hobbes, T. 45
Home Link 127–8
home-school liaison teachers 6, 39
    in Cleveland 32–6
    in Lancashire 36–7
    links with supporting agencies 37, 90,
        93–4
home-school liaison workers 3, 37,
    88–91
home visiting 85–6, 94–5
Hughes, M. 68
Hull, 16, 124
Hulme 125–6
Humour 21, 24
Hunt, J. McVicker 10
Hunt, S. 27, 28, 29, 41
Hunter-Grundin, E. 59, 136

intelligences 117–8
intelligence quota (I.Q.) 10, 13, 116–7
Independent Television (ITV) 19

Jensen, A. R. 117
Joseph, Sir Keith 115

Lancashire Community Relations
    Council 117
Lanchester Polytechnic 58
language:
    English as a second language 64, 74
    spoken 60, 69, 74, 126
    vocabulary 60
    written 60–1

Language and educational disadvantage 12, 71–2
Language and reading development:
    approaches to teaching reading 20, 65
    attitudes to reading 60, 75
    goals and methods 65, 75, 82–4, 75–6
    paired reading 69, 70–71
    'Reading for Meaning' 61
    school policies 73–6
Latin America 48
La Vida 11
Law Centre 94
Leaders 108, 119
Learning
    collaborative 55, 106–9
    continuity in 23
    environment of 10, 121–2
    self-organised 118, 123
    theories of 7
Lee, Laurie 1
Leicester 14, 69, 91
Leicestershire 49
Lewis, Oscar 11, 16
library 58, 94
literacy
    Experimental World Literacy project 48
    Profiles *see* Hunter-Grundin
Liverpool 5, 124
London 4
Lorenz, K. 46
Loughborough 4
love and hate 47

Macintosh, N. J. 116
Macleod, F. 36
Mascie-Taylor, C. G. N. 116
Madeley Court 49
maladjusted children 91
Manchester 2, 16, 18, 26, 124
    local education authority 3
    Polytechnic 2, 5
Mangham, I. 41
Manpower Services Commission 4, 114, 118
Mason, S. 49
McMillan nursery 104
Middleton, N. 7, 114
Midwinter, E. 51
Monitorial system 21
Morris, H. 49
Muslims 117

National Children's Bureau 94
National Society for Prevention of Cruelty to Children 37
Needs assessment 27
Newsom pupils 9
North Hull Neighbourhood Centre 4, 107–8

O-Level 66
Open University 66, 98–9, 107–8, 128
Oxford University 125

Palfreeman, S. 128
parent governors 5, 128–9
parental stances 119–20
parents:
    and teachers 66, 67–8
    and children's groups 79, 95–6
    and personal development 99, 105–6, 115
paternalism 6, 12
Pen Green 109–110
Plowden Report 6, 16, 63
Pink Floyd 118
Pre-school *see* Education, early childhood
Pringle, M. Kellmer 104, 115
professional 74, 121, 130
projects:
    achievement of aims 24–5, 31–2, 128
    management of 92, 99–102, 109, 110
Puerto Rico 12

Racism 42
'Raising Standards' 59
Rampton, A. 42
Raven, J. 68
Reading *see* Language and Reading Development
Relationships 3
Record keeping 100–101
Rennie, J. 58
Rice, M. 103
Robbins Report 9
Russell, B. 47

Salford 4, 69, 91
sanctions 21
Schonell, F. and E. 20
schools:
    democratic decision-making 103–4
    mainstream system 3

  primary 18–20, 78, 79, 82
  secondary 84, 114–5
  special 3, 86–7
  success of 22–4
schools and parents
  contract between 129–30
  consultation of parents 77, 120
  principles of **parental** involvement 2, 4, 16, 31–2, 56, 64
methods 58, 75–6, 78, 80–1, 92–3
Schools Council 2, 63
Secretary of State for Social Services 114
Silver, H. 37
Sharp, R. and Green, A. 15
shop floor university 4
Smallridge, J. 117
Smith, T. 105
Social Science Research Council 115
social workers 30
Stantonbury 49
Sutton Centre 3, 49, 84
Swann report 16, 42–3, 48, 116

Taylor report 128
Telford 49
Thomas, L. F. 118, 121
Tizard, B. 10, 68
Tizard, J. 105
toy libraries 96–7
training
  for professional development 121–3
  inter-disciplinary 121

Urban Aid grants 36
USA 12

Van Leer Foundation 125
Victorian values 18

Walnut Grapevine 82
Warnock, M. 120
Warwick University 58
Watts, J. 49
Weitzman, S. 114
Welling, W. 120
Wells, G. 71
'West Indian Children in our Schools' 42
West Midlands 4
Western Isles of Scotland 64
Westinghouse Learning Corporation 10
Wide Range Readers 20
Wilkinson, A. 12

Yale University 10
Young, M. and McGeeney, P. 14

Zeitgeist 14
Zelan, K. 69
Zigler, E. and Valentine, J. 10, 104